Yeats

Open Guides to Literature

Series Editor: Graham Martin (Professor of Literature, The Open University)

PETER FAULKNER

Yeats

Open University Press
Milton Keynes · Philadelphia

Open University Press
Open University Educational Enterprises Limited
12 Cofferidge Close
Stony Stratford
Milton Keynes MK11 1BY, England

and

242 Cherry Street
Philadelphia, PA 19106, USA

First Published 1987

British Library Cataloguing in Publication Data

Faulkner, Peter
    Yeats.— (Open guides to literature).
    1. Yeats, W.B.
    I. Title   II. Series
    821'.8   PR5904.T6

    ISBN 0-335-15256-2
    ISBN 0-335-15255-4 Pbk

Library of Congress Cataloging-in-Publication Data
Faulkner, Peter.
    Yeats: The tower and The winding stair.

    (Open guides to literature)
    Bibliography: p.
    Includes index.
    1. Yeats, W. B. (William Butler), 1865–1939—Criticism
and interpretation. I. Title II. Series.
PR5907.F38 1987   821'.8   87–7311
ISBN 0–335–15256–2
ISBN 0–335–15255–4 (pbk.)

Typeset by Quadra Associates Ltd, Oxford
Printed in Great Britain by J. W. Arrowsmith Ltd. Bristol

Contents

Series Editor's Preface

The intention of this series is to provide short introductory books about major writers, texts, and literary concepts for students of courses in Higher Education which substantially or wholly involve the study of Literature.

The series adopts a pedagogic approach and style similar to that of Open University Material for Literature courses. *Open Guides* aim to inculcate the reading 'skills' which many introductory books in the field tend, mistakenly, to assume that the reader already possesses. They are, in this sense, 'teacherly' texts, planned and written in a manner which will develop in the reader the confidence to undertake further independent study of the topic. They are 'open' in two senses. First, they offer a three-way tutorial exchange between the writer of the *Guide*, the text or texts in question, and the reader. They invite readers to join in an exploratory discussion of texts, concentrating on their key aspects and on the main problems which readers, coming to the texts for the first time, are likely to encounter. The flow of a *Guide* 'discourse' is established by putting questions for the reader to follow up in a tentative and searching spirit, guided by the writer's comments, but not dominated by an over-arching and single-mindedly-pursued argument or evaluation, which itself requires to be 'read'.

Guides are also 'open' in a second sense. They assume that literary texts are 'plural', that there is no end to interpretation, and that it is for the reader to undertake the pleasurable task of discovering meaning and value in such texts. *Guides* seek to provide, in compact form, such relevant biographical, historical and cultural information as bears upon the reading of the text, and they point the reader to a selection of the best available critical discussions of it. They are not in themselves concerned to propose, or to counter, particular readings of the texts, but rather to put *Guide* readers in a position to do that for themselves. Experienced travellers learn to dispense with guides, and so it should be for readers of this series.

This *Open Guide* is best used in conjunction with *The Collected Poems of* W. B. *Yeats* (Macmillan, 2nd edition 1950 and frequently reprinted). Page references in the *Guide* are to this edition.

Acknowledgements

I am greatly indebted to Graham Martin and the Open University Press for inviting me to write this book, and for helpful comments on the first draft. I am grateful to Mr Michael Yeats and Macmillan and Company, London and New York, for extracts from *A Vision* and *The Letters of W.B. Yeats* ed. Allan Wade, and for the illustrations to the Irish Tourist Board for 'Thoor Ballylee', to Mr Michael Yeats and the National Library of Ireland for the reproduction of the manuscript of 'Easter 1916', to the Municipal Gallery of Modern Art, Dublin, for Max Beerbohm's 'Mr. W.B. Yeats . . .' and to the British Broadcasting Corporation for 'Yeats giving a broadcast'.

1 Yeats and Modern Poetry: His Development

Yeats is now rightly considered in relation to Ezra Pound and T. S. Eliot, the founding fathers of modern poetry in England, especially as the author of *The Tower* (1928) and *The Winding Stair* (1933), on which this Guide is focused. But he differed from Pound and Eliot in at least two important ways: he was not an American but an Irishman, and he was of an older generation, born in 1865, twenty years before Pound and twenty-three before Eliot. The first of these circumstances meant that his subject-matter and perspective, with their basis in Ireland, were quite different from theirs; the second that he began writing while the late Victorian form of Romanticism, as practised most attractively by Tennyson and the Pre-Raphaelites, was still the principal poetic mode. Its influence, making for a lush and vague suggestiveness, can be seen in much of Yeats's early poetry from *The Wanderings of Oisin*, a mythic Irish hero, (pronounced Usheen) in 1889 to *The Wind among the Reeds* in 1899 (though here the influence of French Symbolism may also be discerned).

However, Yeats was never entirely satisfied with this kind of poetry. Looking over the material assembled for his first volume, he wrote to his friend Katharine Tynan: 'it is not the poetry of insight and knowledge, but of longing and complaint – the cry of the heart against necessity. I hope some day to alter that and write poetry of insight and knowledge.'[1] It was because he saw that Yeats was trying to 'modernise' his poetic style in the early years of the twentieth century that Pound was attracted to him when he came to London in 1908. But at that period Yeats's style still seemed old-fashioned to many young writers, and even his 1919 volume *The*

Wild Swans at Coole was dismissed by John Middleton Murry as 'a swan song. It is eloquent of final defeat.'[3] T. S. Eliot's review of Yeats's critical essays *The Cutting of an Agate* in the same year was entitled 'A Foreign Mind', and included the remark that 'Mr Yeats's mind is a mind in some way independent of experience'[3] – an interesting judgment to which we will return. But the publication of *The Tower* in 1928 produced a much more positive response. The American poet John Gould Fletcher wrote in *The Criterion* – the magazine edited by Eliot – that: 'He [Yeats] corresponds, or will correspond, when the true literary history of our epoch is written, to what we moderns mean by a great poet.'[4] When the young F. R. Leavis published *New Bearings in English Poetry* in 1932, he referred to the author of *The Tower* as having achieved 'a difficult and delicate sincerity, and extraordinarily subtle poise',[5] making him suitable for inclusion in a book mainly supporting the achievements of Eliot and Pound. When *The Winding Stair* was reviewed in *The Criterion* in 1934, Hugh Gordon Porteus emphasised how Yeats had transformed his early attitude: 'Yeats . . . has plumbed the depths of romanticism; but although he still employs a romantic idiom (it is part of his programme, and he knows what he is doing), he brings to it now a vision astonishingly refined and disciplined'.[6] In *After Strange Gods* in the same year T. S. Eliot was praising the austere power of Yeats's poetry, 'his arrival, against the greatest odds, at greatness.'[7] At the time of his death in 1939, the leading left-wing poet of the next generation, W. H. Auden, was to write of his diction as showing 'a continuous evolution towards what one might call the true demoncratic style. . . . The diction of *The Winding Stair* is the diction of a just man'[8] – and, by implication, that of a recognisably *modern* poet.

I share the belief that it is in his later poetry that Yeats found an appropriately modern style in which to express his response to life with great authority, and so this Guide is focused on *The Tower* and *The Winding Stair*. I think you will also find that the many recent critics who think highly of Yeats's achievement tend to refer most frequently to poems like 'Sailing to Byzantium', 'The Tower', 'Leda and the Swan', 'Among School Children', 'A Dialogue of Self and Soul' and 'Byzantium', all to be found in these two volumes.

However, in order to gain some sense of the developing mind of the poet, I suggest that you now read four of Yeats's early poems, in chronological order, and try to formulate for yourself a sense of their characteristic features. Of course, any small representation of an author's work like this runs the risk of being misleading, but I hope that you will find something interesting to work on. The poems I suggest are:

'The Stolen Child', from *Crossways*, 1889, p. 20;
'The Lake Isle of Innisfree', from *The Rose*, 1893, p. 44;
'The Valley of the Black Pig', from *The Wind among the Reeds* 1899, p. 73;
and 'The Folly of Being Comforted', from *In the Seven Woods*, 1903, p.86.

(a) 'The Stolen Child' is an appealing and apparently simple poem based on the common folk-story of the child who is stolen away into the land of the fairies – in the Irish context, that of the Sidhe (pronounced Shee). (Yeats has a Note on the Sidhe on p. 514.)

What impression of the Sidhe do you obtain from the poem? What is their attitude to the child? Does it change or develop interestingly? Now read the poem.

DISCUSSION

Here is my impression of it; I hope it overlaps with yours.

The evocative description of the countryside, that of the Sligo neighbourhood on the West Coast of Ireland where Yeats spent much of his childhood, and the account of the mischievous exploits of the Sidhe, combined with the ballad effect of the chorus – 'Come away, O human child' – seem to me to create an atmosphere of glamour and at first the reader is led to feel that the child is being taken away for his or her own good to a happier world. The poem becomes more complex with the last stanza where, when the child is actually leaving the human world, the Sidhe admit the existence of attractive aspects of it which have hitherto been ignored or repressed, so that their final triumphant chorus – 'For he comes, the human child' – seems to the reader to express a sense of success which is not really concerned about the child's future happiness. The theme of the comparative value of the world of ordinary human experience as against some higher or more beautiful world of the imagination is, as we shall see, one to which Yeats frequently returned. Here it is dramatised in an attractive Irish context – without, I think you will agree, any great feeling or urgency.

This, incidentally, is the poem to which Yeats was specifically referring in his letter about 'longing and complaint' referred to above (p. 1).

(b) 'The Lake Isle of Innisfree' is one of the most popular and frequently anthologised of Yeats's poems. Why do you think that is? By the time that it was written, Yeats had moved with his family to London.

Do you think this is relevant to the poem? Now read the poem.

DISCUSSION

You will notice that it evokes a beautiful countryside similar to that in 'The Stolen Child', but this time we have a first-person narrator, evidently an exile in a city, who is feeling the strongest sense of home sickness, a common experience in our modern world of rapid and frequent movement. The beautiful picture which the poem creates in the first two stanzas is obviously idealised (no effort goes into the making of the 'small cabin' or the cultivation of the bean-rows). Nevertheless, the open vowels of 'the bee-loud glade', the changing colours of the second stanza, the serenity yet liveliness suggested by 'the evening full of the linnet's wings', have a strong appeal to many of us who respond to the attractive idea of 'getting away from it all'. The final stanza reveals the intensity of the narrator's longings by referring explicitly to his separation from the beautiful world he has been describing. We can see the source of the poem in Yeats's own experience, but the quality of the vision created in all its romanticism is what chiefly impresses us.

(c) 'The Valley of the Black Pig' is obviously a different kind of poem, with a mythological emphasis suggested by the mysterious title. The note provided by Yeats on pp. 526–7 refers to prophecies of the eventual defeat of the enemies of Ireland, but ends by seeing the Battle as mythological and the Pig as Winter fighting Summer, or Death fighting Life.

What kind of battle do you find in the poem? What do you make of the 'flaming door' with which it ends? Now read the poem.

DISCUSSION

What the poem itself evokes is surely a sense of mysterious dreams and sudden awakening from them into a world of battle, but battle of an archaic kind with spears and horsemen. The poet associates himself with those who 'labour by the cromlech [a prehistoric stone structure] on the shore', who are evidently seeking some kind of higher reality than that of 'world's empires'. These are prepared to worship an unnamed spiritual power who is described in the mysterious final line of the poem as 'Master of the still stars and of the flaming door'. The reader feels on the edge of another world, perhaps to be approached through the 'flaming door' which may suggest a kind of purgatorial experience. In this poem we have moved away from the landscape of Ireland to mythology, although a mythology with Irish associations.

(d) 'The Folly of Being Comforted' feels like a more direct rendering of experience in terms of a dialogue. Whose voices do you hear? How do you understand the conclusion? Now read the poem.

DISCUSSION

First we hear the voice of a kind friend remarking on the signs of age in the poet's 'well-beloved' and counselling patient acceptance. But the reply comes not from the expected narrator, an 'I' to correspond with the 'you' of the first section, but from the dramatised Heart, which refuses any comfort. Even though her nobility means that she retains her vitality, presented in the imagery of fire, Heart feels that nothing can compensate for the changes since the days of youth – 'wild summer'. The final couplet of the poems is addressed to the Heart by the elusive narrator, and is surely ambiguous. Maybe her turning her head would confirm Heart in its sense of irreparable loss; but more interesting is the suggestion that Heart would in fact be comforted – after all, she is still 'the well-beloved' – but would also be aware of the folly involved in accepting comfort. Do you think that this is reading too subtly? I think it is justified, as we are dealing here with a poet well into his career, and with great ambitions. The poem is more personal and dramatic than those we have previously considered, partly because of the use of the dialogue form.

Now read four more poems, again in chronological order, from Yeats's middle period, again remembering that no small selection of this kind can be really representative:

'No Second Troy', *The Green Helmet and Other Poems*, 1910, p. 101,
'September 1913', from *Responsibilities*, 1914, pp. 121-1,
'An Irish Airman foresees his Death', from *The Wild Swans at Coole*, 1919, p. 152
and 'Easter 1916', from *Michael Robartes and the Dancer*, 1921, pp. 202–5.

What developments do you see?
(e) 'No Second Troy' is directly concerned with a woman. She has evidently caused the poet to suffer, but is apparently not to be blamed for this. Why not? How would you describe the tone of the poem? What do you make of the image of the 'tightened bow'? What is the point of the reference to Troy? Now read the poem.

DISCUSSION

This is another dramatic poem, though we hear only one voice, that of the poet discussing the woman who has caused him to suffer.

(You may know enough of Yeats's life to think of Maud Gonne.) The poem does not blame the woman, but rather the times in which she is living. If she has caused revolutionary violence – which we will link with the Irish nationalist struggle against England – and caused the poet sufferings, this is simply because she is a heroic figure whose archaic qualities find inadequate expression in the modern world. The image of the 'tightened bow' surely suggests tension and danger, and leads forward to the suggestion in the final line that the woman is the successor of Helen, whose beauty had led to the destruction of Troy. Here Yeats is leading the reader onto the plane of heroic legend and myth to which his imagination was powerfully attracted, and which we encountered in 'The Valley of the Black Pig'. A marked feature of the poem is of course the series of urgent questions which helps to create the dramatic feeling and bring the heroic past into a vivid relationship with the contrastingly unheroic present.

(f) 'September 1913' is a poem with the feel of a ballad about it, deriving mainly from the memorable 'chorus' lines about Romantic Ireland and O'Leary. It differs from its predecessors in its more specific references to Irish political leaders. John O'Leary (1830–1907) was a Nationalist whom Yeats had known and admired; Lord Edward Fitzgerald (1763–98) led the 1798 Rising; Robert Emmett (1778–1803) was executed for leading another rebellion; Wolfe Tone (1763–98) took part in the 1798 Rising and killed himself while under sentence of death. The 'wild geese' of stanza 3 were Irishmen who emigrated after the Treaty of Limerick in 1791, and often served in continental armies from the eighteenth century onwards. What is the overall mood of the poem? How do you understand the phrase 'that delirium of the brave'? Now read the poem.

DISCUSSION

I think you will agree that the mood is angry and bitter. The poet is contrasting the impulsive and courageous Nationalist leaders of the past with modern Irishmen – the date in the title emphasises this – who are concerned only 'to pray and save': to save their souls by 'shivering' prayers – the adjective suggesting their abject cowardice – and to get as much money as they can. The sacrifices of the past heroes seem pointless if they have led only to the materialistic, selfish state of the Ireland of 1913, in which notions of self-sacrifice are so remote that the heroes' behaviour would now be regarded as mad romanticism. What if perhaps in part it was? The phrase 'all that delirium of the brave' seems to admit that possibility. By the end of the poem, though, the surviving feelings are of reluctant acceptance ('But let them be . . .'). There is no point in trying to retain the notions of the heroic in modern Ireland. The poem expresses complete disillusionment, but does so with striking vigour.

(g) 'An Irishman foresees his Death' is another first-person narrative. The airman is associated with Kiltartan, the area near Coole Park, the home of Yeats's friend and patron, Lady Gregory. This poem follows 'In Memory of Major Robert Gregory'. Robert Gregory (1881–1918) was Lady Gregory's only child, and was killed on the Italian front while serving with the Royal Flying Corps. What effect is achieved by the reference to Kiltartan? How does the tone of the poem contribute to our understanding of the airman's point of view? Now read the poem.

DISCUSSION

The airman is evidently Irish, but he has been fighting in a war unlikely to affect Ireland – the Great War of 1914–1918, in which aircraft first played a signficant part. The airman is expecting to die in battle, in a war about whose outcome he shows little interest. But he is by no means a sad figure. The tone of the poem is surely joyful; death is accepted as 'my fate'. The emphasis is on the airman's motives for participating in the war, which are certainly not the usual ones – law, duty, public men, cheering crowds, all are dismissed as irrelevant. His association with Kiltartan and its poor distances him from the politics of the war, which do not concern him. The usual motives are negated until we come to the positive assertion: 'A lonely impulse of delight/Drove to this tumult in the clouds'. The airman is a kind of existentialist hero, fighting not to produce results but for the satisfaction of the activity in itself; indeed, fighting is not referred to in the concluding part of the poem. It is as if the airman is subjecting himself to a test, to see how he can cope with the 'tumult', and this is for him an 'impulse of delight', lonely because it must be experienced by and for an individual, but producing delight out of danger and indeed, as the final word emphasises, out of death itself. The argument of the poem is surprising, but it is conducted in a brisk manner, enforced by the simple rhyming,and admitting no doubts.

(h) 'Easter 1916' is a more elaborate poem, and also one which directly arises from historical events. It is hardly intelligible without some knowledge of the Easter Rising which took place in Dublin in

1916, when Yeats himself was in England. Up to the outbreak of World War I in August 1914, the Liberal Government had been seeking ways of giving Ireland its constitutional independence, despite the powerful resistance of the British Conservative Opposition and the Ulster Unionists. The Home Rule Bill was passed in September 1914, but was immediately suspended for the duration of the War. The Nationalists believed that the War was being used as an excuse for avoiding action, and also that it provided an excellent opportunity, while British forces were occupied elsewhere, to take the military initiative. A small group of Nationalists (the names of several of whom appear in the poem) led a rising, which they hoped would spread; they took the Post Office in Dublin, but had little other success. However, the British authorities took a very tough line, executing the sixteen leaders, and this naturally aroused very strong anti-British feelings throughout Ireland.

What attitude to these events do you find presented in the poem? Do you find it complex? Consider in particular the third section ('Hearts with one purpose alone . . .'). Now read the poem.

DISCUSSION

In the first section the poet thinks back to his acquaintance with the leaders of the Rising as he had known them earlier, in a world of 'polite meaningless words': suddenly everything is changed: 'A terrible beauty is born'. This paradoxical phrase (technically an 'oxymoron' when the two words 'terrible' and 'beauty' apparently contradict one another) brilliantly expresses a complex response to the events, and the excited surprise of the poet at finding that heroic action is still possible in a world which (as 'September 1913' showed) he had come to think of as incapable of heroism. The second considers some of the leaders of the Rising; whatever their various personal characteristics, they have now been 'transformed utterly'. The third section deepens and complicates the poem by looking more closely at what is involved in their transformation: it has involved turning hearts, symbols of life and energy, into stone. The poem leaves behind this sombre reflection on what has been sacrificed by these heroic leaders – their very humanity? – to urge 'our part', the reader's responsibility, shared with the poet, which is to 'murmur' the names of these new heroes, to recall their deeds whether politically productive or not ('For England may keep faith . . .'). The transformation, whatever its human cost, has occurred, and Irishmen will forever remember those who took part in this decisive act. Again, the confident manner of the poem brooks no argument.

We have now read and discussed a small number of Yeats's earlier poems from 1889 to 1919. What impression do you have of his poetic development? You may find it helpful to re-read the poems and our discussion of them before formulating your views.

I imagine that your overall feelings about the poet's development will be that he had a continuing preoccupation with Ireland (although of course also with other themes), but that the later poems suggest a more 'realistic' approach, one that focuses less on landscape and mythology and more on social and political elements – and that there is a related change of style, particularly evident in the diction (choice of words), which becomes more colloquial, and the rhythm, which becomes more dramatic in the sense of suggesting a living voice or voices. The early work is more obviously 'poetic', creating its own world out of legend and dream. One epigraph to the 1914 volume is: 'In dreams begins responsibility'. This is attributed to an old play, but is probably an invention. It suggests the new direction which the poet's work was taking. However, there is a second epigraph from the *Analects* of the Chinese sage Confucius: 'How am I fallen from myself, for a long time now I have not seen the Prince of Chang in my dreams.' The Prince was an author and statesman, and this may be read as an affirmation that although the poet is accepting his responsibility to speak directly about contemporary life, he also acknowledges the need for the guidance and inspiration that dreams can give. Yeats was a great admirer of the visionary poet and painter William Blake, and – as we have already seen – was often concerned to express the tension between the facts of experience and the power of the imagination. Indeed, a tension of this kind may be seen as a common factor in all the poems we have so far looked at. Do you agree? Or do you feel that to make a generalisation of this kind is to misrepresent the exciting variousness of the poetry?

Perhaps this would be a good point at which to offer some background information about the poet's life and times prior to the volumes of 1928 and 1933 on which this book will concentrate.

2 Yeats's Life and Times

William Butler Yeats was born in Dublin in 1865. His father was a young lawyer with a talent for painting; his mother was from the family of a ship-owning merchant of Sligo on the West Coast, where Yeats spent many of his early holidays. For in 1867 the family moved to England for J. B. Yeats to pursue a career as portrait-painter; three other children were born, the youngest Jack to become an important Irish painter. However, in 1880 they came back to Dublin. On leaving school in 1883, Yeats refused to go to Trinity College, preferring to become an art student. But by now he had begun writing poetry, and he came to see that he had more talent for writing than for painting.

In 1887 the family moved back to London, and Yeats made every effort to publish his work. He became a reviewer and literary journalist, publishing anthologies of Irish writings, and met distinguished writers like the Socialist William Morris, the Imperialist W. E. Henley and the aesthete Oscar Wilde. He already knew the old Nationalist leader, John O'Leary, who introduced him to the beautiful Maud Gonne, with whom he fell, unrequitedly, in love. Despite rejection, he remained devoted to her, and she is the subject of much of his love poetry. He also joined the Theosophical Society, and was initiated into the Hermetic Order of the Golden Dawn. I mention these very diverse facts and people in order to show the diversity of Yeats's early involvements. If we find complexity in his poetry, it may be related to his vigorous and interested responses to such diverse influences.

His first volume, *The Wanderings of Oisin and Other Poems*, was, as we have seen, published in 1889; it did not attract much attention. However, the 1890s saw a developing interest in the non-English cultures of the British Isles, which came to be known as the

Celtic Twilight; Yeats published a volume of that name in 1893
containing a number of folk stories. In 1891 he founded the Irish
Literary Society, and he worked on a three-volume edition of the
poetry of Blake, published in 1893, in connection with which he
pursued the study of symbolism, so important for his poetry. The
evidence of this is to be found in his two volumes of the decade, *The
Rose* (the lyrical poems from *The Countess Kathleen and Various
Legends and Lyrics*), 1893, and *The Wind among the Reeds*, 1899,
with their many uses of the rose and other symbols.

In 1896 Yeats was introduced to Lady Augusta Gregory, the
wife of an Anglo-Irish diplomat who had a country residence at
Coole Park, Ballylee. She became a great friend and an encouraging
patron, and Yeats was to spend several summers from 1897
onwards living and writing at Coole Park. Lady Gregory encouraged Yeats's interest in folk-lore, visiting with him the homes of her
tenants and listening to their stories. She also encouraged him to
work for the theatre, work which led him in 1902 to the founding
of the Irish National Theatre Society, with the Irish actor Frank Fay
as its leading theatrical figure. In 1904 the financial support of the
English philanthropist and theatre enthusiast Florence Horniman,
well known in Manchester, made possible the opening of the Abbey
Theatre. When this was reorganised more professionally in 1906
Yeats became a director together with Lady Gregory and J. M.
Synge, a playwright whose works and personality Yeats greatly
admired. In 1907 Synge's *The Playboy of the Western World*
provoked outrage among Nationalist theatre-goers for its allegedly
upatriotic depiction of the Irish in comic terms; Yeats defended the
play, but was becoming increasingly aware that his literary and
artistic ideals were not widely shared by his Nationalist fellow-
countrymen. His disillusion with contemporary Ireland, by contrast
with the pre-Christian, warrior society of such heroes as Cuchulain
on which he based his own plays, led him into a number of
controversies which found powerful expression in the small volume
Poems written in Discouragement in 1913. This included 'September 1913'. The poems were reprinted in the following year in the
larger volume *Responsibilites*, the title of which may be seen as
claiming a new area of public activity for the poet who had
previously been largely associated with the esoteric and mythological.

Simultaneously, as we have seen in looking at some of Yeats's
poems in chronological order, Yeats had been changing his poetic
style away from its early gentle Romanticism towards something
more dramatic – his association with the theatre in these years is
highly relevant. In one of a series of short essays called *Discoveries*,

'Mr. W.B. yeats presenting Mr. George Moore to the Queen of the Fairies'; cartoon by Max Beerbohm, 1904.

1906–7, (to be read now in *Essays and Introductions*), Yeats
vividly describes the two possibilities which seem to him to be open
to poets at this time: either to continue in the Romantic Symbolist
tradition predominant especially in French poetry, or to try to
create something less ethereal and more fully human. This is how
he describes the situation and the choice. Do you feel that he is
recommending one course?

> In literature, partly from the lack of that spoken word that knits us
> to normal man, we have lost in personality, in our delight in the
> whole man – blood, imagination, intellect, running together – but
> have found a new delight, in essences, in states of mind, in pure
> imagination, in all that comes to us most easily in elaborate music.
> There are two ways before literature – upward into ever-increasing
> subtlety ... or downward, taking the soul with us until all is
> simplified or solidified again. That is the choice of choices – the way
> of the bird until common eyes have lost us, or to the market
> carts. . . .[1]

It seems to me that although Yeats states the antithesis fairly
enough, he is himself keen to move towards what he calls 'the
market carts', symbols of ordinary life. The idea of an integrated
and integrative poetry in which 'blood, imagination, intellect' work
together to express 'the whole man' became central to Yeats. The
idea may usefully be compared with T. S. Eliot's account in his
essay 'The Metaphysical Poets' in 1921 (to be read in his *Collected
Essays* or Frank Kermode's *Selected Essays of T. S. Eliot*) of the
'dissociation of sensibility' in the seventeenth century; this had led
to a supposed separation between thought and feeling in the poetry
of the Romantics and Victorians. D. H. Lawrence was also to
emphasise the need for humanity not to suppress those elements of
the personality suggested by the word 'blood'. For Yeats it was the
work of Synge, who died young in 1909, that expressed this coarse
but necessary vitality, without which literature would become
ethereal and of no interest to ordinary people.

The development of Yeats's style towards greater tautness and
dramatic force was encouraged by his friendship with Ezra Pound.
Pound had come to England in 1908 and soon established himself
in literary London as a powerful influence for change, advocating
'The New' in poetry, fiction, painting, sculpture and music. Yeats
saw a good deal of him in 1912, and Pound became his unofficial
secretary for a while. In addition to encouraging Yeats to develop a
more 'modern' style, Pound was also responsible for introducing
him in 1915 to the Japanese Nōh plays. In this stylised form of
drama, with its masks and dancing, Yeats found a valuable
alternative to the naturalistic drama of playwrights like Lennox

Robinson and Sean O'Casey; to Yeats's regret, this drama was proving more popular at the Abbey Theatre than his own plays or those of Synge. He now began experimenting with short plays in an idiom derived from the Nōh, the first of which was *At the Hawk's Well*, 1916.

Meanwhile, the Easter Rising in Dublin (already mentioned in relation to 'Easter 1916') had recalled Yeats to a new sense of his Irishness. In 1917 while on a visit to Coole Park, he found a broken-down Norman tower at Ballylee and decided to buy it for his Irish home. In his private life a series of events took place which from an outside point of view border on farce: Maud Gonne's estranged husband, John MacBride, (whom she had married in 1903), had been executed for participation in the Easter Rising; Yeats again proposed to Maud, she again rejected him, and then to her step-daughter, Iseult, who also rejected him. But in the same year, 1917, he was accepted by Georgie Hyde-Lees, whom he married in the autumn of that year. During their Sussex honeymoon, Mrs Yeats attempted automatic writing; Yeats was greatly excited by the messages reaching him so unexpectedly, and set out to formulate a mystical philosophical system to embody them. This found expression in a number of poems – like the dialogue between Hic and Ille called 'Ego Dominus Tuus' and that between Aherne and Robartes called 'The Phases of the Moon', and 'The Double Vision of Michael Robartes', all in *The Wild Swans at Coole*, 1921; and eventually too, in the prose work *A Vision*, first published in 1925. Meanwhile two children were born, Anne in 1919 and Michael in 1921. For each of these a fine poem was written: 'A Prayer for My Daughter' and 'A Prayer for My Son'.

Affairs in Ireland had reached a violent stage. In December 1918 the separatist Nationalist party Sinn Fein, led by Eamon de Valera, won a sweeping election victory. Its members declined their seats at Westminster, convened the Dail (Parliament) in Dublin, and in January 1919 declared that Ireland had seceded from the United Kingdom. This meant war with England, led in Ireland by Arthur Griffith and Michael Collins, who organised the Irish Republican Army for that purpose. The British brought in the Black and Tans, an army which was composed of ex-Servicemen from World War I and which rapidly gained a reputation for brutality. Yeats returned to Dublin in 1920 and worked in the Nationalist cause, publishing 'Easter 1916' together with the more anti-British poems 'Sixteen Dead Men' and 'The Rose Tree' – the latter suggesting that only the 'red blood' of the leaders executed in 1916 could nourish the Rose Tree of Irish Nationalism. Lady Gregory was also writing vigorously for the cause in a paper called *The*

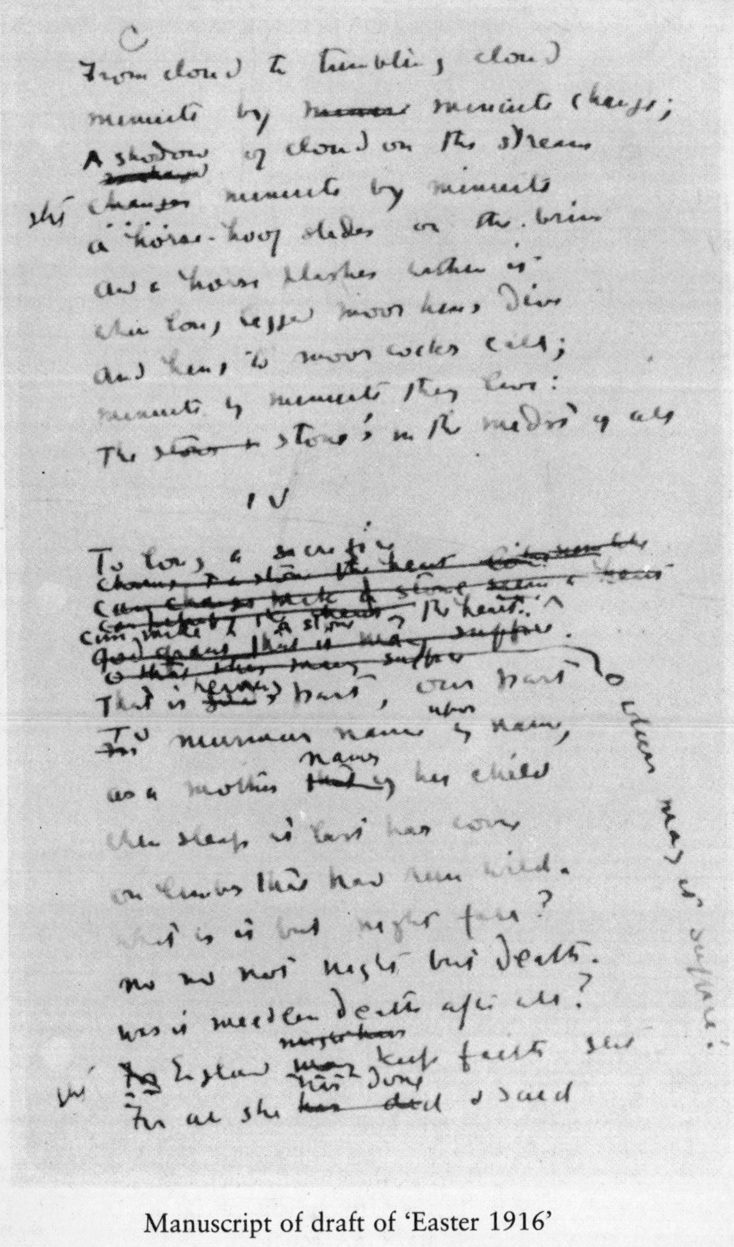

C

From cloud to tumbling cloud
minute by minute changes;
A shadow of cloud on the stream
Changes minute by minute
A horse-hoof slides on the brim
And a horse plashes within it
Where long-legged moor-hens dive
And hens to moor-cocks call;
minute by minute they live:
The stone's in the midst of all

IV

To long a sacrifice
Can make a stone of the heart.
That is heaven's part, our part
To murmur name upon name,
As a mother names her child
When sleep at last has come
On limbs that had run wild.
What is it but nightfall?
No no not night but death.
Was it needless death after all?
For England may keep faith
For all that is done & said

O when may it suffice?

Manuscript of draft of 'Easter 1916'

Nation; in November 1920 she wrote an article entitle 'Murder by the Throat' concerning the shooting at the gate to her house of Ellen Quinny, a pregnant mother with three children. Yeats was to refer to the incident in 'Nineteen Hundred and Nineteen', as we shall see. He also denounced British policy in a powerful speech at the Oxford Union.

In July 1921 a truce was proclaimed, and in December a Treaty was signed between the British and Irish governments granting the Irish Free State the status of a Dominion but not a Republic; Ulster would however be allowed to remain in the United Kingdom if it voted to do so. This led to the complicated and dangerous situation that we have in Ireland today. But many Nationalists wanted to go further towards the establishment of a totally independent Republic which would include Ulster, and refused to take the required Oath of Loyalty to the Crown. They were led by de Valera. The Dail accepted the Treaty by 64 votes to 57, but Civil War broken out in July 1922. Griffith, who became President, died of a heart attack in August, Collins was killed in an IRA ambush. Yeats favoured the Treaty, but tried to remain neutral; he was also deeply distressed by the violence. In a letter dated 21 October 1922 he wrote movingly: 'The one enlivening Truth that starts out of it all is that we may learn charity after mutual contempt. There is no longer a virtuous nation and the best of us live by candle light.'[2]

The end of the Civil War in 1923 saw a precarious peace. Yeats accepted the post of Senator in 1922, and worked hard for the next six years to try to build a united and civilised Ireland. Yeats was awarded the Nobel Prize for Literature in 1925, and was an active member of the Senate, making powerful speeches on divorce in 1923 and on the dangers of the Copyright Bill in 1927. He was disturbed by the growing evidence of repressive clerical influence at work in the Free State, making particularly difficult the position of those like himself who felt no allegiance to the Roman Catholic Church. There was no possibility for a writer like James Joyce, who had exiled himself from Ireland in 1904 and published *Ulysses* in 1922, to return to this 'new' Ireland in which his work was considered obscene as well as blasphemous. In late 1927 Yeats's health broken down, and Mrs Yeats took him to Spain, and then to Cannes. In February 1928 he moved along the coast to Rapallo (by now the home of Ezra Pound), then briefly back to Dublin, before returning to Rapallo in October to convalesce. He no longer had the energy to pursue his work in the Senate.

3 The Tower

The Tower, published in February 1928 by Macmillan in London, consists of poems written between 1919 and 1927, that is to say, before Yeats's illness. The poem entitled 'Nineteen Hundred and Nineteen' is dated 1919, and the final poem in the volume, 'All Soul's Night' had been published in *The London Mercury* in March 1921.[1] The first poem, 'Sailing to Byzantium', is dated 1927. All the poems but one had appeared previously in the small editions published by the Cuala Press in Dublin, *Seven Poems and a Fragment* (1922), *The Cat and the Moon and Certain Poems* (1924), and *October Blast* (1927). The only previously unpublished poem is 'The Gift of Harun Al-Rashid', which was later placed among the 'Narrative and Dramatic' poems at the end of the *Collected Poems* as we now have them, as a result of which it is little read. In 1933 Yeats slightly changed the order of the poems and added the brief 'Fragments'; he also cut down the poem 'The Hero, the Girl and the Fool' to its final section, 'The Fool by the Roadside'. The full poem can be found in R. J. Finneran's edition, *W. B. Yeats: The Poems, A New Edition* (1984). Some of the implications of these facts will be discussed later. Here it is necessary simply to emphasise that the poems in *The Tower* were written during the years of Ireland's emergence into nationhood, and of Yeats's greatest involvement in public affairs.

Three Major Poems

We will begin our reading of the volume by looking at three of its most elaborate and impressive poems, 'Sailing to Byzantium', 'Among School Children' and 'All Souls' Night'. These are all complex poems, especially the first two, and will repay many readings, but for the moment I suggest that you simply try to identify the central theme in each and formulate your general impressions, not dwelling too much on particular allusions or difficulties.

'Sailing to Byzantium'

Let us begin with the first poem. I suggest you read it fairly quickly, to get the sense of the developing action. What kind of voyage does the poet make? How important do the diction and imagery make the voyage seem? How does the poem develop in both action and tone?

DISCUSSION

I hope you will have experienced a sense of definiteness and authority about the manner of the first two stanzas, modifying into a kind of prayer in the third and returning to confident statement, though about the future, in the final stanza. The poet is confronting the problem of ageing with verve and determination.

How is this effect produced?

Partly by the diction, partly by the syntactic flow, by the choice of the formal eight-lined stanza known by the Italian name *ottava rima*: regular rhyme, ababab (young/trees/song/seas/long/dies), though Yeats does not insist on perfect rhymes – the off rhymes of 'young' and 'song' and of 'seas' and 'dies' contribute to the effect of natural speech – followed by a clinching couplet (neglect/intellect).

The first stanza begins with a simple statement. It then goes on to evoke the life of the country, from which the old man feels alienated, in a vigorous, flowing sentence of over five lines, full of natural imagery linked to the season of summer. The word 'dies' – referring back to 'Those dying generations' – is a reminder to the poet of what is the underlying reality, but it does nothing to disturb the young 'In one another's arms'. They are said to be 'Caught in that sensual music', the word 'caught' implying a trap, that of mortality, of which they are unaware. Finally an alternative is offered: 'Monuments of unageing intellect'. The sculptural image supersedes the musical in the search for something beyond the cycle of natural change, and 'intellect' is offered as opposed to the senses enjoyed in the world of the young.

The second stanza focuses on the condition of age, in the undignified image of the scarecrow. But again there is an alternative: 'Soul', strikingly personified in human terms, can transcend its own condition, its 'mortal dress' of the body, clapping and singing in an ecstasy which it can teach itself by studying the 'Monuments of its own magnificence'. The alliteration here contributes to the effect of authority, and, through the reference back to the end of the previous stanza, allies the soul with the 'unageing intellect' in the assertion of super-sensual values. The final couplet flows smoothly, and confidently; the poet has chosen his course and carried it out successfully; he has now reached 'the holy city' where transcendental values prevail. (We will consider the choice of Byzantium as the city thus sought at a later stage in our discussion.)

The third stanza is addressed to some un-named sages who stand in 'God's holy fire' in a world of perfection like that represented in the 'gold mosaic of a wall' in a Byzantine church (in which the floors were decorated with animals or fishes, the walls with human personages, and the ceilings with higher beings). The sages are asked to come and 'be the singing masters of my soul' — continuing the reference to the 'singing school' of the soul's monuments in the previous stanza, teaching the higher wisdom which the ageing man needs. The phrase 'perne in a gyre' is perhaps puzzling at first, though we may well be familiar with the relevant and related word 'gyrate'. 'Perne' is a dialect word based on a memory of Sligo speech, referring to the spool on which thread is wound, 'Gyre' is a more learned word (which Yeats pronounced with a 'g'), defined in the *OED* as 'A turning round, revolution, whirl; a circular or spiral turn'. It was an important word to Yeats, who develops the ideas associated with it in *A Vision*. (Again, we will defer further consideration so as not to lose our sense of the poem's unfolding action.) The intensity now increases as the poet asks to enter into a purgatorial experience; the rapid movement over the line-endings helps to create the note of anguish at the bewilderment of the heart at finding itself 'fastened to a dying animal', the human body. The stanza, however, ends with a confident appeal to be 'gathered' — a protective, even maternal word — 'Into the artifice of eternity'. This is a striking phrase, and at first seems to suggest an achieved perfection beyond time. But on further consideration we may feel a qualifying doubt. Isn't there something rather hard, even sterile, about being gathered not into arms but into an artifice? Even if it is that of eternity? It depends which of those two words is given the greater emphasis. It is more appropriate to what has gone before that we should emphasise the final word, 'eternity'.

The fourth stanza goes on to meditate on that eternity by stating confidently that 'Once out of nature' — that is to say,

presumably, dead, – the poet will not take his 'bodily form from
any natural thing'. There is a suggestion of the idea of reincarnation
here, with the poet refusing to remain within the natural order.
What can he chose instead? The last six lines of the poem move
eloquently to an answer: he can choose a form such as that created
in Byzantine art with its splendid use of precious materials (note the
repetition of 'gold' as noun and adjective): he can be an artificial
bird, for what other creature do we expect to see on a 'golden
bough' singing to the court? Now he is part of 'the artifice of
eternity', splendid and valuable, singing forever to the Emperor and
his 'lords and ladies'. The 'birds in the trees' of the country of the
young in the first stanza have been superseded by a splendid
artefact.

Before we try to bring our responses to the poem into a
conclusive form, let us return to two points that we passed by
rapidly on our first reading: the choice of Byzantium as the 'holy
city' of the voyage, and the idea of the gyre. Both of these relate to
material in *A Vision*, the strange book first published in 1925 (there
was to be a revised edition in 1937), in which Yeats tried to put into
orderly shape the ideas that had come to him in his wife's automatic
writings. He wished to make these the basis for an Idealist
philosophy.

Most of us probably know, or can find from reference books,
that Byzantium (later Constantinople and now Istanbul) became
the capital of the Eastern Empire when Constantine transferred his
court from Rome in the fourth century. The art which developed
there showed powerful Eastern influences, marked by the architec-
tural use of the round arch, cross, circle and dome, and by rich
mosaic work employing gold and precious stones. Yeats was
fascinated by these artistic achievements (he saw a number of such
mosaics in Italy and Sicily in 1925), which he saw as antithetical to
the humanistic styles of ancient Greece and of the Renaissance. His
mind throve on such antitheses. The appeal for him of Byzantium
may be seen from the account of it which he gives in *A Vision*. This
is a perplexing book for those of us not well-versed in esoteric
wisdom, and it is important to stress that reading it is as likely to
bewilder as to enlighten; certainly if you read it in the hope of
finding 'the key' to Yeats's poetry you will be disappointed. This is
not to say that the book is irrelevant, but that it needs careful
interpretation – and that poetry is a richer and more complex
discourse than explanatory prose. Despite these caveats, it is worth
looking at Yeats's remarks on Byzantium, which he considers in
Book V, 'Dove or Swan', in giving an account of history. He argues
that sometime in the fifth century 'Byzantium became Byzantine

and substituted for formal Roman magnificence, with its glorifica-
tion of physical power, an architecture that suggests the Sacred City
in the Apocalypse of St John'. He sees it has been a uniquely unified
culture:

> I think that in early Byzantium, maybe never before or since in
> recorded history, religious, aesthetic and practical life was one, that
> architect and artificers – though not, it may be, poets, for language
> had been the instrument of controversy and must have grown
> abstract – spoke to the multitude and the few alike. The painter, the
> mosaic worker, the worker in gold and silver, the illuminator of
> sacred books, were almost impersonal, almost perhaps without the
> consciousness of individual design, absorbed in their subject matter
> and that the vision of a whole people.[2]

He would have liked, he fancifully suggests, to have spent a month
there: 'I think I could find in some little wine-shop some
philosophical worker in mosaic who could answer all my questions,
the supernatural obviously nearer to him than to Plotinus even
. . .'[3] Plotinus was a Neoplatonic philosopher of the second
century, to whom we shall find further references.

How significant is this information in relation to the poem?

Only partially, I think, which should act as a reminder that
what goes on inside a poem or other work of art must be looked at
in its own terms. *A Vision* shows us how much Yeats valued the
culture of Byzantium for its spiritual and artistic unity, and this
evaluation contributes to the poem; but the rather William-Morris-
like emphasis on the unity of art and civilization, with the workers
conveying a living tradition in their artefacts, remains unused in the
poem, where the artefacts are isolated from their makers.

The second area in which *A Vision* may be helpfully – if
carefully – invoked is that concerned with the idea of the gyre,
referred to in stanza 3. In Book I of *A Vision*, 'The Great Wheel',
Yeats sees all existence in terms derived from the Greek philosopher
Empedocles, as a continual tension between the forces of Discord
and Concord, whose contrary movement forms an ever-whirling
vortex. He provides a diagram and commentary on the interpene-
trating vortices:

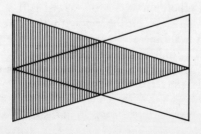

If I call the unshaded cone 'Discord' and the other 'Concord' and
think of each as the bound of a gyre, I see that the gyre of 'Concord'
diminishes as that of 'Discord' increases, and can imagine after that
the gyre of 'Concord' increasing while that of 'Discord' diminishes,
and so on, one gyre within the other always. Here the thought of
Heraclitus dominates all: 'Dying each other's life, living each other's
death.'[4]

All this may seem to be taking us a long way from the request to the
sages to give their saving wisdom to the suffering soul, but is it
more difficult or obscure than other forms of philosophical or
religious language? Some readers find Yeats's world too private,
but in the poem that dramatic situation remains perfectly clear. The
term is used with more complex implications elsewhere, most
strikingly in the opening poem of the 1938 volume, *New Poems*,
which is entitled 'The Gyres'.

Let us now return to the ending of the poem, and ask how
satisfying it is. Does the protagonist seem to have reached a
successful conclusion? Certainly the structure and flow of the
poetry suggests that he has. Just as stanza 2 ended with a sense of
the relaxed completion of the voyage, stanza 4 ends with a parallel
suggestion of a spiritual journey reaching tranquillity. And yet we
may not feel altogether satisfied. However hard the poet tries to
convince himself of the superiority of Byzantium to the vigorous life
of youth, something in him undermines his own efforts: the text
seems to contradict itself. What do you think of the following
objection to the conclusion of the poem? It was offered by the poet
and friend T. Sturge Moore (who had designed the cover of the
volume) in a letter to Yeats at the time:

> Your 'Sailing to Byzantium', magnificent as the first three stanzas
> are, lets me down in the fourth, as such a goldsmith's bird is as much
> part of nature as man's body, especially if it only sings like Homer
> and Shakespeare of what is past or passing or to come to Lords and
> Ladies.[5]

The criticism impressed Yeats, who told Moore that it stimulated
him to write 'Byzantium'[6] in 1930 – a poem we shall be discussing
later. I find the objection excessive – a goldsmith's bird does *not*
seem to me 'as much part of nature as man's body' – but it does
draw attention to a real problem with the poem's conclusion.
Surely there is something anti-climactic about the final picture we
are left with? The golden bird may be a remarkable artefact, but its
audience is not very interested if the 'drowsy Emperor' is typical;
and its song (like that of all literature, as Sturge Moore's comment
suggests) is about the very life which it wants to leave behind. Thus
in the telling phrase of F. R. Leavis in his essay 'Yeats: the Problem

and the Challenge', 'Intensely the soul interrogates itself and its images of fulfilment and finds no answer that doesn't turn into an irony.'[7]

'Sailing to Byzantium' is nevertheless an assured and splendid poem on one of the central themes of Romantic literature. You may see a parallel with Keats's consideration in the 'Ode to a Grecian Urn' of the relationship between the transience of life and the permanence (it would be more accurate to say, durance) of art. If Yeats's poem does not finally settle the problem, it is because it is one of those central human problems which can never be permanently settled. And I would want to argue that a good deal of the vitality of the poem (note that I naturally find myself using a word closely associated with life rather than art at this point) is attributable to the unresolved tension between the feeling for youthful life expressed in the first stanza and the anguished need to find something better, expressed in the third. The poem remains a 'monument' for us, but one in which the commendation of sensuousness is memorably heard.

'Among School Children'

Now read this poem, which occurs about half way through the volume and is written in the same *ottava rima* form. How does it strike you by comparison with 'Sailing to Byzantium'? Can you discern a central theme and a developing line of argument? How do you understand and respond to the powerful and challenging questions at the end?

DISCUSSION

I expect you will have been aware of a more direct sense of autobiography in its opening, and possibly a different direction to its ultimate argument. Instead of the symbolic holy city of Byzantium or even the generalised country of the young, we enter the poem in a realistic scene with Senator Yeats carrying out one of his public duties and visiting a progressive convent school (actually in Waterford). Critics have differed over the attitude to the kind of education described here: do you find the tone ironical? I don't: it seems to me that the atmosphere is relaxed and agreeable, the children undisturbed by their important visitor. Yeats approves of 'the best modern way' represented here. The tone is humane and acceptant.

And yet, of course, as stanza 2 shows, the poet is not fully concentrating on the school-room. The 'I walk' of stanza 1 is replaced by 'I dream', and the poetry now becomes more urgent, as the rhythm is broken at the line-endings – each of the first three lines involves running over into the next. A 'Ledaean body' is an important phrase, relating the child being dreamed of – whom we can assume to be Maud Gonne in view of the presentation of her in earlier poems like 'No Second Troy' – to Helen of Troy, born of the rape of Leda by Jupiter in the form of a swan (the subject of the previous poem but one). The stanza evokes a scene of 'youthful sympathy', the young people talking to each other about their schooldays and finding a total unity as they talked together. Two images of their unity are offered: the sphere, attributed to Plato, and the more down-to-earth image of 'the yolk and white' of an egg. This duality fits the emerging argument of the poem, which is, as we shall see, concerned with Platonic and alternative ways of seeing reality.

Stanza 3 shows the poet looking at the girls in the schoolroom and wondering whether his unnamed beloved 'stood so at that age', and this thought causes him great excitement: now 'She stands before me as a living child'. The concluding rhyme makes this an authoritative statement, with the result that we may fail to notice how extraordinary it is. The poet's imagination is triumphant over time and circumstance.

In stanza 4 'Her present image' is contrasted with the imagined sight of the no-longer-existent girl, and it is the former which 'floats into the mind', the verb, 'floats' giving it a spectral quality: the present is less powerful than the past. Yet it is reality, however disturbing, and the reference to the painting of the Italian Quattrocento (fourteenth century) suggests a certain kind of hollow-cheeked ethereal beauty a long way from youthful vitality. The poet even thinks that *he* was once handsome, but abandons this fruitless thought. It is better to smile back to those who smile at the ageing man, and show that he can bear the process of ageing without complaint. The scarecrow image reminds one of 'Sailing to Byzantium', but here the poet is trying to avoid bitterness.

Stanza 5, however, shows that bitterness is hard to avoid, though it looks at the ageing man from a different perspective, that of the mother. Are the sufferings of women in childbirth compensated for by such a 'shape with sixty or more winters on its head?' The implied is clearly negative.

In stanza 6 we encounter three famous philosophers, who might be expected to be able to answer the difficult questions so far raised about human identity and worth: Plato the Idealist, dismissive of nature; 'Solider Aristotle', more of a materialist, but remembered here as the tutor of Alexander the Great, whom he no doubt punished with 'the taws' [a Scots word for a schoolmaster's leather strap] (the tone is comic – it is almost as if Aristotle is proving, as against Plato, the solidity of material objects by caning his pupil); and Pythagoras, the mathematician and astronomer, who believed in the music of the spheres – a music unable to rouse the interest of the 'careless Muses'. The stanza concludes with a line which returns back to the imagery of Stanza 4; it dismisses all three philosophers as no more than scarecrows. Their ideas, however philosophical, have failed to save them from the humiliations of the ageing body.

The last two stanzas run powerfully together, and are the most difficult, as well as the most impressive, part of the poem. The transition to stanza 7 is abrupt. Why are we in the world of 'nuns and mothers'?

The answer takes us back to stanza 5, and suggests that mothers are able to survive the sufferings of labour because they are sustained by an image of the child which they can worship just as a nun is sustained by contemplating the 'repose' of a statue (though no nun would actually admit to worshipping an image). The fifth line, beginning 'And yet they took break hearts', implies that all worship of this kind is an attempt to go beyond the human: after the broken heart, there may be peace. However, this kind of peace is repudiated in the ecstatic vision to which the poem now moves with great rhythmical power – partly achieved by the movement over the stanza ending. The poem now addresses these representatives of 'heavenly glory' known to 'passion, piety, or affection' – respectively the emotions of lover, nun and mother – which in their self-born perfection mock 'man's enterprise' (a phrase with an element of the pun about it: man's enterprise is simply to live, but to do that takes nerve and courage).

The splendid stanza 8 begins with a declaration about a state of perfect being in which 'labour' – Adam's curse, but also that of mothers, in both cases involving effort and suffering – is transformed into 'blossoming or dancing', two evocative images of vital beauty. In this state all the usual antinomies of human existence, which Yeats so often experiences as insoluble, are actually resolved: the body is not sacrificed to the soul, beauty is not created from despair, wisdom is not won by arduous toil. This is a paradisal state, but the imagery of nature makes it an earthly paradise. The poem ends with two rhetorical questions, addressed to the two images of the first line, the implied answer to which assumes unity of being. The tree is a whole living creature, the blossom inconceivable without the great roots; the dancer in the dance is an indissoluble unity. Once the dance is over, the figure that emerges is no longer the dancer, only an ordinary human body.

The figure of the dancer is an important one in late nineteenth-century culture, as Frank Kermode showed in *Romantic Image* in 1957. Kermode puts it neatly:

> There is a tormenting contrast between these images (signified by the bronze and marble statuettes) and the living beauty. And out of the contrast grows the need for a poetic image which will resemble the living beauty rather than the marble or bronze. No static image will now serve; there must be movement, the different sort of life that a dancer has by comparison with the most perfect object of art.[8]

This would suggest that the poem ends with a satisfying and convincing assertion of value. Not all readers have felt this, however. The American critic Yvor Winters, a great debunker of Romanticism, remarked adversely: 'The body is always bruised to pleasure soul; wisdom is always born out of midnight oil or something comparable.'[9]

Now read the poem again. Do you agree with Winters? His remark has an element of grim truth about it, but it seems to deny the right of the poet to use his imagination to create images of perfection, which is surely one of the pleasures that literature and art can give. I find my response much closer to that of F. R. Leavis, in the essay previously quoted, who sees the climax of the poem as coming with 'a perfect cogency of musical logic.'[10]

Which commentator — Winters or Leavis — best reflects your own view? Leavis goes on to claim 'There is nothing else like that in the collected poems',[11] but we can return to that assertion when we have considered a wider range of the poetry.

Finally, is the poem related to 'Sailing to Byzantium'?

Although, as we have seen, they employ the same verse form and have a similar quality of authority about them, they move in opposite directions as far as the thought goes. Instead of looking for an ideal 'out of nature', 'Among School Children' finds its solution to the dichotomy between the children and the ageing man of its first stanza in the contemplation of an ecstatic natural harmony.

'All Souls' Night'

The final poem in the volume, dated 'Oxford 1920', is an elaborate poem in ten ten-line stanzas, in which the poet tries to summon and address the spirits of the dead, after midnight leading into the day in November dedicated in the Roman Catholic Church to prayer for the faithful departed who are still suffering in Purgatory. Yeats had used the poem to conclude *A Vision* in 1925, and in keeping with the unorthodox thought of that work, he avoids any commitment to Christian doctrine. What he is conducting is more like a séance than a service. What line of development do you find in the poem? Are the characters who are referred to in stanzas 3 to 8 made vivid and significant? What do you notice about the conclusion?

DISCUSSION

The opening stanza creates an atmosphere of midnight mystery, leading to the suggestion that 'A ghost may come' to 'drink from the wine-breath', while the 'gross palates' of the living consume the muscatel itself. The poet is seeking an audience, the second stanza tells us, 'Because I have a marvellous thing to say' – something so remarkable that the living mock at it, and he therefore seeks to impart it to a mind that can, however bad things may be in the world, retain its serenity; 'stay/Wound in mind's pondering/As mummies in the mummy-cloth are wound'. The simile, referring to Egyptian burial customs, gives a strange physicality to 'mind's ponderings', a physicality which enables them to protect and enclose the mind itself. The last two lines, about the likely effects of hearing the 'marvellous thing', suggest that it would have a powerful emotional effect, carrying its hearers beyond normal sobriety.

The next six stanzas are devoted to summoning three appropriate spirits from among Yeats's dead acquainances: William Thomas Horton (1864-1919), a painter and illustrator of mystical scenes, notable to the poet for the intensity of his Platonic love which made a single image out of God and his dead beloved, and turned heaven, in an amusing and unexpected simile, into a goldfish-bowl containing only one splendid fish; Florence Farr Emery (1869-1917), an actress who had worked in the Irish Literary Theatre with the young Yeats, and who left England in 1912 to teach in India – she is celebrated in the sixth stanza for her knowledge of esoteric wisdom concerning the journey of the soul towards the 'delight' of liberation; and MacGregor Mathers (1854-1918), one of the founders of the occultist Order of the Golden Dawn to which Yeats belonged in the 1890s, and with whom he had quarrelled in 1900 over Order matters. The poet now forgivingly views Mathers' strange mental attitude as the product of his devotion to 'unknown thought', but amusingly sees Mathers' ghost as retaining enough of his old cantankerousness to 'object to the host' – perhaps, indeed, he 'may have grown more arrogant being a ghost'. This ability to see matters associated with the occult in an unexpectedly realistic or even cynical way is an attractive characteristic of Yeats's writings about a subject which often provokes excessive solemnity.

Here I should like to raise a question of considerable general importance. I have given some biographical information about the three people referred to in the poem. How valuable did you find it? Was it essential for your understanding of the poem? Would you agree that the poem itself provides all that it is *essential* to know; dates and facts do nothing to improve the vivid portraits provided in the text, although we may reasonably welcome the information as confirming the impression we have been given. I suggest that this is usually what we find in Yeats's poetry: allusion, certainly, often to people and events in his own experience, but given significance and substanital presence within the text itself. His allusions are less esoteric than those of Pound and Eliot, and it is an error of judgement to divert to biographical study the energy which produces exciting results when devoted to actually reading the poems with care.

The last two stanzas – like those of 'Among School Children' – rise towards ecstasy. 'Names' are dismissed as 'nothing': all that matters is that those summoned are spirits with finer 'elements' than those of the living, who therefore constitute the audience he wants for the 'mummy truths' he has to tell. Note how the earlier reference to how 'mummies in the mummy-cloth are wound' has led to this striking phrase; what do you think it implies? Surely that the truths of the esoteric tradition to which Yeats, like his three dead friends, to some extent belongs are hidden from the living but nevertheless preserve their fineness. The last stanza achieves its sense of ecstasy largely because of its rhythmical energy: the repetition of 'such thought' (which gives rise to a strange but persuasive syntax) helps to sustain the sweep of the sentence into two parts separated by a semi-colon. The first six lines affirm the power of vision given by the 'thought' ('Nothing can stay my glance . . .') to pierce beyond the material world to those of the spirits of the damned and the blessed, and the confidence of the poet in the value of his 'thoughts', which give him complete security, like that of the 'mummies in the mummy-cloth'. His achieved attitude is one of serenity: 'I need no other thing'.

This strikes me as a powerful and successful poem, but you may have noticed an interesting omission. Does the poem reveal the 'marvellous thing' that the poet tells us he has to say? If not, why not?

DISCUSSION

My answer would be 'No'. The poet has apparently been playing a game with the reader, who finds himself with no information to enable him to share the poet's serenity at the end of the poem. But we may on reflection decide that there is good reason for the apparent omission, and this lies in the central argument of the poem. The reason why the reader is not told the 'thought' is that he or she is one of 'the living' and so too coarse, too crude, too human, to be able to appreciate it. The poet himself, in the course of the poem, has become a spiritualised voice, and so left us behind in 'the world' he despises, while he achieves the security of his spiritual confidence.

So what has the reader been offered if not the 'thought'?

Surely the answer is: the experience of the poem, of seeing the poet spiritualised himself – almost before our eyes? It is doubtful whether poetry can convey spiritual doctrine: that is the task of theology. What poetry can convey better than other forms of writing is a sense of *experience*, in this case the experience of a powerful imagination finding security in the spiritual. Whether or not we share the poem's confidence in spirituality in our ordinary lives, while reading the poem we are powerfully led to do so. The concluding affirmation of 'All Souls' Night' brings *The Tower* to an authoritative end.

The three poems we have been reading show Yeats writing with authority about some of his major preoccupations: the problem of ageing, the relations of soul to body, and of art to nature. They all employ a formal stanza and conventional syntax, but also give us a vivid sense of the speaking voice in their diction and in their strikingly effective shifts of register from the formal to the colloquial.

They are also clearly concerned with important ideas, many of them expounded in *A Vision*. What is it that makes these ideas into poetry? As we saw in Chapter 1, Yeats wanted to express 'the whole man – blood, imagination, intellect running together'. I believe that he achieves this unity in these poems, in a variety of ways. In 'Sailing to Byzantium' we are aware of a mainly symbolic method; in 'Among School Children' and 'All Souls' Night' there is a stronger sense of the autobiographical mode, with the constructed 'I' of the poem narrating events and feelings to which we respond. In these poems too the imagery – the chestnut tree, the dancer, the mummy-cloth – carries much of the significance. We shall find these methods in other poems in the volume, as well as the use of *personae* (dramatized figures narrating the poems) and of the ballad-form which we encountered in the earlier poetry. A volume like *The Tower* employs many different poetic strategies, and we must be on the lookout to identify them as we read.

'The Tower' as a Sacred Book

Now we have looked at the three poems with some care, do you notice any connection between them? What significance do you see in the dates supplied by Yeats for the first and last poems?

It seems to me that there is an obvious continuity of theme, especially between 'Sailing to Byzantium' and 'All Souls' Night', but also including 'Among School Children'. All three are philosophical poems concerned with the question whether anything permanent can be discovered to console Man (or, a man) for the sufferings of life and the inevitability of death. In each case consolation is found, twice in what we have been terming spirituality, and once in ecstatic contemplation of natural process. It may occur to you that when the poems are put together in this way, the conclusion of 'All Souls' Night' is less attractive than it seemed when we were considering the poem on its own terms. Compared with the splendid affirmative energy of the chestnut tree and the dancer, isn't there something almost comically reductive about both the golden bird of 'Sailing to Byzantium' and the complacent self-mummification of 'All Souls' Night'? You may not agree, but putting the poems together makes it possible to raise such relevantly interesting issues.

It also perhaps gives us an inkling of the way in which Yeats created a volume of poetry. Unlike, say, Thomas Hardy, whose numerous poems appeared in various volumes arranged in the most casual ways, Yeats clearly planned each volume. The three poems we have considered, in some ways the most elaborate, are deliberately placed, despite the chronology of their writing, as opening, centre and conclusion. And as you read further in the volume, you will, I think, see further relationships.

Some of these relationships have been entertainingly suggested by the American critic Hugh Kenner in an article entitled 'The Sacred Book of the Arts' (1956). The first part of the article, 'Catechism', is in the form of a discussion between Q, evidently a teacher, and A, evidently a student (the letters wittily suggesting a whole Socratic teaching strategy). It begins:

Q: In 'Among School Children' we read of a 'Ledean body'. Where are we to seek information about that?

A: Not from the mythological dictionary, but as, everybody knows, from the poem 'Leda and the Swan'.

Q: And where is this poem to be discovered?

A: On the previous page.[12]

This leads to a consideration of the non-chronological ordering of the poems, and to A's noticing that the volume 'gets more and more deliberate as one examines it. He begins the volume by renouncing his body; he ends it in the possession of disembodied thought'.[13] The volume is now seen to be 'a dramatic progression', the presence of which, 'once . . . discerned, modifies all the parts'. This is surely a most helpful assessment, in the light of which we may now proceed to look at other poems.

Please now read through the whole volume in an exploratory way, gaining an overall sense of it without dwelling too long on any single poem. Consider whether your reading experience confirms Kenner's suggestion that there is 'dramatic progression', or leads you to some other view of the relationship between the various poems. I have used Kenner's thesis to structure the comments that follow, but you should approach these comments in a questioning frame of mind.

The volume begins with four substantial poems: 'Sailing to Byzantium', followed by 'The Tower', 'Meditations in Time of Civil War', and 'Nineteen Hundred and Nineteen'. The last three of these have in common that each is divided into a number of sections. These poems are therefore rather more diffuse than the concentrated, undivided poems so far studied. The reader is challenged to see the reasons for the ordering of the material and the connections between the different sections. (We have encountered something similar before in connection with the relationship between stanzas, especially in 'Among School Children', but here the question is made more obvious.)

What do you take to be the central theme of 'The Tower'? Do you see any connection with the preceding poem, 'Sailing to Byzantium'?

DISCUSSION

'The Tower' opens colloquially in a vigorous address to the poet's heart about the problem of age. It clearly thus relates in theme to 'Sailing to Byzantium', but now the 'I', using colloquial language, seems closer to ordinary reality, and so to events in the poet's life. The vigorous movement of the rhyming ten-syllable lines, not divided into stanzas, conveys an urgent concern about the poet's present plight: he is an ageing man, but his imagination and senses are more active than ever before in his life. Indeed, 'ear and eye' now expect 'the impossible' – a striking way of exposing the vitality of his senses, but perhaps also suggesting an unrealistic extra-vagance of attitude. However that may be, he is faced with an unpleasant choice: he can either 'bid the Muse go pack' and cultivate instead philosophy, represented by Plato and Plotinus, who 'deal in abstract things' and can help the poet to do so too – which means losing his capacity for imaginative and sensuous experience; or he can continue to enjoy these at the expense of being 'derided' by his awareness of the ageing of the body, expressed in the powerful because unexpected and vivid image of the 'battered kettle' tied to a dog's tail.

Let us now consider the poem in greater detail.

The first part is brief and dramatic, and it leaves the problem open. The second is longer and more leisurely, containing thirteen stanzas with a simple rhyme scheme, aabbcddc, which gives a sense of order. The poet paces 'upon the battlements'. We are reminded of the poem's title, that of the volume too; evidently the tower is a physical reality, whatever symbolic quality we may feel it becomes invested with. Again, biography is useful, but the poem embodies a coherent meaning in itself. Yeats's own Note (pp. 532–3) refers us to 'Thoor Ballylee or Ballylee Castle, where the poem was written'. You will perhaps recall, from the biographical section (p. 14), that Yeats had bought the Norman tower at Ballylee as part of his search for his Irish identity, and he had it done up as his home after his marriage. Now he 'sends' his 'imagination forth' to call 'Images and memories' from the locality, to which he refers in his Note: Mrs French, whose butler cut off the ears of an 'insolent farmer'; 'peasant girl', Mary Hynes, and the blind poet Raftery who celebrated her; Hanrahan, the hero of Yeats's own fiction *Stories of Red Hanrahan* (1904), who had pursued a 'phantom hare and hounds' (and, although the poem does not reveal it, ended his life in madness after the failure of his quest for perfect beauty, perhaps similar to that created in imaginative poetry by blind poets like Homer); a previous bankrupt owner; men-at-arms of earlier periods whose ghosts still appear to sleepers in the house. All these are summoned to answer a question arising from the problem of Part I: did they all, 'rich and poor', being old, 'rage/As I do now against old age?' No direct answer is given, however. What do you think the poet sees in the 'eyes/That are impatient to be gone'?

I suppose that the answer is so obviously 'yes' that it is hardly worth giving, though conceivably the question is not as significant to the dead as it is to the living.

The poet allows the others to leave, but retains his own creation, Hanrahan, to whom he addresses another, very different, question:

> Does the imagination dwell the most
> Upon a woman won or woman lost?

It seems that the first question is now no longer so significant; what matters concerns the imagination, and the question of what stimulates it. Again, no direct answer is given, but the poet seems to be forcing Hanrahan to answer 'lost', and then to 'admit' both that he had 'turned aside/From a great labyrinth' – presumably 'the labyrinth of another's being' referred to in the previous stanza – for whatever reason, and that, climactically, 'if memory recur, the sun's/Under eclipse and the day blotted out'. As usual with Yeats, this is a rhetorically effective ending, but what exactly does it mean? In conjunction with previous imagery linking the sun to ordinary life and vision, and the moon to imagination, it evidently means that the operation of imaginative memory of the 'woman lost' would wipe out everything else and become the only significant reality.

How does this relate to the first part? I see it as a refusal by the poet to surrender his imagination, an assertion of its power, even if that imagination is not to become 'content with argument'. Can the third and final part of the poem resolve the problem, which remains unsolved by an affirmation of imagination that simply ignores the ageing of the body?

Part III is written in shorter, six- or seven-syllable lines, with a good deal of rhyme. This gives a speedy and resolute effect, in keeping with the poet's decisive state of mind. He has come to a conclusion, and can make his will, leaving his pride to 'upstanding men', fishermen, representatives of human energy and skill. The reiteration of the word 'pride' and the series of unexpected similes used about it, culminating in the reference to the last song of the dying swan, give the quality a strong positive value. This quality is overtly associated with a particular group of people – 'people that were/Bound neither to cause nor State . . . The people of Burke and of Grattan/That gave, though free to refuse'. Here we find a theme not previously encountered, that of passionate commitment to the tradition usually described as Anglo-Irish or the Protestant Ascendancy, from which Yeats's father's descended.

Here we need help from scholars about Yeats's relationship to the tradition. Edmund Burke (1729–97) was the great eighteenth-century political writer whose *Reflections on the Revolution in France* (1790–1) gave powerful expression to the Tory view that society must evolve 'naturally', and not by revolution, while Henry Gratton (1746–1820) was a great orator and Irish parliamentarian. (Ireland had had its own Parliament before the 1801 Act of Union.) This Anglo-Irish tradition is particularly well evoked by T. R. Henn in Chapter 1 of *The Lonely Tower* (1949).[14]

It was represented for Yeats both by his own family and a number of friends, including in particular Lady Gregory of nearby Coole Park. Henn writes:

> Before the First World War that aristocratic culture seemed to have given so much: pride of race, independence of thought, and a certain integrity of political values.[15]

Henn's phraseology echoes 'The Tower'. The independence and integrity Yeats valued – perhaps exaggerated – were the products of a class standing in a unique relationship to Ireland: English in origin and culture, educated – if male – at Oxford, Cambridge, or Trinity College, Dublin, Protestant in religion, but staunchly Irish, in their own way, in commitment and values. It was with this independent position that Yeats tried to align himself in the Irish Senate, though getting increasingly isolated as Catholic Nationalism asserted itself in the later 1920s. (All this is fully and fairly discussed by Elizabeth Cullingford in her *Yeats, Ireland and Fascism* (1981), especially Chapter 7 'In Time of Civil War' and Chapter 10 'The Senate'.)

So here we find a kind of political or nationalist commitment which could obviously find no place in the more philosophical poems discussed earlier, but which we shall encounter often again. But what does it contribute to 'The Tower'?

Consider your own view before reading on.

Through the invocation of will and inheritance the poet places himself directly in a particular society, several elements of which had been evoked in the previous part of the poem. Evidently his sense of himself as part of the Anglo-Irish tradition, and the pride that he feels in this, enable him to achieve the confidence of his new declaration of faith, in which he dismisses Plato and Plotinus – the 'friends' towards whom he seemed to be pushed in the opening part – with great élan. Instead of accepting their transcendentalism, to which man is subordinate, the poet asserts a kind of humanism: it is man who created 'Death and life . . . Out of his bitter soul'. The sun, moon and stars, often used to symbolise a divine order, are human creations, and man is even able to go beyond death:

> . . . being dead, we rise,
> Dream and so create
> Translunar Paradise.

(*OED:* Translunary: 'Lying beyond or above the moon . . . ethereal, insubstanial, visionary.' Yeats would no doubt have preferred the last term.)

This is an extraordinary affirmation, based on faith in the human ability to dream – that is to say, in the human imagination. But you may feel that the idea is merely asserted rather than made fully convincing.

After this assertion the poetry becomes quieter; appropriately, for the poet is discussing how he has made his peace in preparation for death. He has done this by resorting to art (Italian and Greek), poetry, imagination, memory, all the activities in which humanity creates, in a striking phrase, 'a superhuman/Mirror-resembling dream'. 'Superhuman' seems immediately appropriate; but why 'mirror-resembling'? My tentative suggestion is that the dream resembles a mirror because it is a version of reality, but nevertheless a strange and self-enclosed world at the same time. But it is a difficult idea. Do you have any other suggestions?

The poem concludes with three fairly short, quite colloquial sections. In the first we are given an attractive picture of a maternal jackdaw. This takes us unexpectedly back to the scene on the battlements of the tower – not mentioned since the opening of Part II – and is congruous with the poet's re-locating himself in physical reality. He asserts again in the next section that his legacy of 'faith and pride', the qualities dominating the earlier lines of this part, will go to 'young upstanding men' such as he was before devoting himself to the exhausting labour of poetry. 'Now shall I make my soul' opens the final section. This comes with simple confidence. He has seen that the imagination offers in art and vision something more valuable than the 'abstract things' and arguments of philosophy, and he will resort to the imaginative tradition, which is nevertheless 'a learned school'. (We may associate it with the 'Monuments of unageing intellect' of the previous poem.) The length of the final wandering sentence beautifully conveys the achievement of serenity. Old age, so threatening in part I, has now lost its sting. Death will come gently, accepted as part of the natural course of things. The ending is less triumphant here than in the other poems, but effective in its quiet humanity.

The title of the next poem-sequence, 'Meditations in Time of Civil War', dated 1923, takes us into the chaotic political situation in Ireland immediately after the acceptance of the Treaty with

England in 1922, which provoked the resistance of the Republicans led by De Valera (see Chapter 2, p. 16 above).

Read the poem again now. Do you see any relation to the preceding poems?

DISCUSSION

It begins with a section, 'Ancestral Houses', which moves with a dignified meditative slowness as it ponders the values represented by the great houses of the Anglo-Irish aristocracy, many of which were destroyed at the time. The tone is detached, argumentative. The first stanza evokes a civilised and leisurely way of life, free from 'ambitious pains', symbolised by the fountain (though isn't there something disturbing about the use of what seems in context to be a man-made fountain as a symbol of life taking its own shape, free from interference?). Belief in this way of life is dismissed – 'Mere dreams' – but it is nevertheless asserted that the artistic imagination can operate only in the belief that some such energy is potential in humanity. However, in the modern context 'an empty sea-shell', something left behind by history, seems a better symbol than the fountain.

The third stanza argues that the houses were created by violent bitter' men seeking to create in stone a sweetness and gentleness antithetical to their own natures. But maybe the descendants are degenerate – 'but a mouse' (reductively rhyming with 'house'). This leads to the powerful question which runs through the eight-line sentence constituting the fourth stanza: what if all the elegance of these creations of civilisation paradoxically destroys the values it was built to embody, taking 'greatness' away as it converts the 'violence' into art? (Note how effectively in this and the following stanza Yeats evokes a sense of eighteenth-century order and formality, using devices of eighteenth-century poetry like the personification of 'slippered Contemplation'.)

The final stanza repeats the paradox with enhanced force, making us reflect upon the disturbing suggestion that bitterness and violence are the necessary spurs to the creation of civilisation. The effect is increased by the use of the first person plural, 'our greatness', 'our bitterness'. This would suggest an ironic philosophy of history, moving between the poles of violence and civilisation. But in this context it may contain the positive suggestion that the violence of the present may ultimately prove creative, or the spur to creation.

After this, the poem becomes more personal – the titles of the next five sections all include the word 'my'. 'My House' gives a vivid sense of Thoor Ballylee set in its 'acre of stony ground' among elms and thorns, exposed to rain and wind, but still a place where 'the symbolic rose can break in flower'. 'Break in' rather than 'break into' gives an uncomfortable sense: nothing is easy here. We then enter the tower, ascend the winding stair, find ourselves in a chamber with writing and a candle, which is compared to the one in which the Platonist in Milton's poem *Il Penseroso* (The Thoughful Man) explored his idea of the power of the imagination as 'daemonic rage'. The last three lines effectively conflate the imaginary with the real – it is as if the candle seen by local travellers has been that of Milton's creation rather than the real Yeats. The final stanza concerns the founders of the tower. The original founder was apparently a soldier who took refuge there with his men in times of war (like the present), but he is presented in a negative way, as leader of a group of 'castaways/Forgetting and forgot'. The second 'founder' is Yeats himself, who restored the tower for habitation and sees it as offering to his heirs the kind of emblem of adversity which will 'exalt a lonely mind'. For Yeats 'lonely' is usually a positive term; he admires the kind of mind which is self-sufficient, and will be stimulated not dismayed by an image like that of the tower, here not the phallic symbol of Freudian psychology but an image of the human effort to create even amid the least propitious circumstances – or perhaps, to go back to the paradox of 'Ancestral Houses', *especially* then.

'My Table' employs a more apparently casual form, rhyming couplets of eight or six syllables. It celebrates 'Sato's gift', the Japanese ceremonial sword given to the poet by Junzo Sato in March 1920, the product of a long unbroken tradition of creative skill. It also obviously represents a martial tradition, perhaps comparable to that of the Anglo-Irish.

This section is brisk and, to my mind, difficult. Each sentence is clear, but their relationship problematical. The sword has remained unchanged over the years, its changelessness a function of man's 'aching heart', aware of change. The tradition was passed on unchangingly too, and its inheritors came to share 'the soul's unchanging look'. But the 'most rich inheritor' of the tradition (presumably rich primarily in an imaginative sense) was so aware of change and of the value of art that, despite his impressive external manner, he 'Had waking wits'. Why is this emphasised? Presumably the implication is that, unlike his predecessors for whom the tradition had become a mere convention, he was fully aware – or perhaps was close to madness? The phrase does not seem explicit enough, nor do the concluding line and a half, although vividly dramatic, clarify the situation: 'it seemed/Juno's peacock screamed'. The peacock was sacred to the goddess Juno as a symbol of immortality. In *A Vision* Yeats states that its scream symbolises the end of a civilisation.[16] No doubt that is relevant here. The unchanging beauty of the sword contrast with the changing phases of civilisation. It lies on the poet's table as a reminder of these complex interconnections.

'My Descendants' is a more formal section, in three eight-line stanzas. It meditates on the possibilities of heredity, without confidence. The descent into 'common greenness' strikes a strong anti-Nationalist note. His descendants (the children are already described as 'a woman and a man') may 'lose the flower', become degenerate; if so he would like the 'stark tower' to become a ruin again, habitation only for the owl: this suggestion contrasts neatly with the idea of the mouse-like inheritors of the ancestral houses. The third stanza move with regularity and confidence. Even the owls are ordered by a superior power, the Primum Mobile (First Mover) of Ptolemaic astronomy which constitutes the outermost sphere of the cosmos, conveying the spheres of the planets and fixed stars in its daily revolution. If the universe is orderly, the poet can have a firm belief. He gives a movingly human explanation of his work on the tower, bought out of friendship for the 'old neighbour' Lady Gregory, and 'decked and altered' for the love of his new wife, Georgie. Now 'love and friendship are enough' – here is no longing for changeless perfection – and the knowledge that the 'stones' will remain as monuments to that love and friendship, whatever changes may occur, is positive and reassuring.

Section V introduces the Civil War directly (and see Yeats's Note, p. 534). The tower is visited by representatives of both the Republican Irregulars and the Government forces. The poet is obviously impressed by the nonchalance of the joking Irregular; he makes trivial conversation with the government Lieutenant. When they have left, he concentrates on the moor-hen chicks in the stream to silence his envy: a vivid evocation. But why is he envious?

Because these men have popular causes to which they are committed; they act with others; they have no doubts. The poet himself goes back towards his chamber with a great sense of loneliness; the 'cold snows' suggest austerity. How much of an alternative to the active life represented by the soldiers does the imagination provide? The implied answer seems negative.

Section VI is particularly effective, its four stanzas each culminating in the ballad-like appeal to the honey-bees to build their nest in that left empty by the starlings. The natural feeling of the first stanza gives way to the powerful evocation of the violence of the war in the second and third, the sense of confusion – 'no clear fact to be discerned' – and of waste – 'That dead young soldier in his blood'.

The last stanza summarises the errors of the previous years, seen as an emphasis on enmity to England rather than a positive sense of national unity, with terrible lucidity:

> More substance in our enmities
> Than in our love.

It is not irrelevant to reflect here on the disturbing accuracy of this in relation to many other movements of national liberation subsequent to the Irish, as well as to the current Irish situation. The poet's only answer is a kind of prayer to the honey-bees. These creatures have of course a long history as symbols of creativity and constructive action, and they attractively symbolize the spirit which Ireland needs to heal its wounds and lead it to fulfilment, a spirit associated with nature rather than the abstract fantasies which are held to have brutalised the Irish imagination. Here the poet successfully integrates his private experience with the needs of the whole nation.

The last section is strange and disturbing, as the poet climbs to the top of the tower and sees a mist sweeping over the countryside under a sword-like moon. The vision becomes surreal. Angry voices are heard. Yeats's Note (p. 534) tells us that the call for vengeance for the murder of an eighteenth-century Grand Master of the Templars, which 'fed class-hatred' when incorporated into Masonic rituals, seems to him 'fit symbol for those who labour from hatred, and so for sterility in various kinds'. The poetry vividly presents these rageful phantoms, and we feel how it is that the poet almost finds himself joining in the call for vengeance (the spirit of the honey-bees is far away). Then there is a vision of mysterious ladies riding on unicorns; as the title of the section suggests, these represent 'the Heart's Fullness': a condition, evidently, of total self-involvement producing a sterile stillness, the mirror image of the violence of the previous stanza. Then both these groups are superseded by 'brazen hawks', whose presence is given great vividness and power in the repeated negatives ('Nor . . . nor . . . nor . . . Nothing . . .') and the visual impact of the final image when the 'innumerable clanging wings' ('clanging' giving a wonderfully metallic effect – these hawks are 'brazen') have 'put out the moon'. They dominate the whole universe.

Nevertheless there is a sense in which the poet controls these forces. In the final stanza he leaves them behind to wonder about his choice of the poet's life rather than that of a man of action. But the conclusion is positive. He realizes that the satisfaction of wordly success would never have been enough for him. The final sentence is a confident assertion that the poet's vocation still 'suffices' him, as it has always done. He can find satisfaction in an 'abstract joy' – one not derived directly from human experiences – and in trying to read the 'wisdom of daemonic images'. These are what we have just seen in the visions; 'daemonic' they certainly were, coming from a source deeper than that of normal experience, which Yeats feels it is his challenge, and his privilege, to explore, the excitement of which activity fully compensated for the restrictions it imposed.

'Meditations' seems to me a very successful poem; its title and framework means that there is a good deal of freedom to explore various aspects of the situation both personal and social without having to seek a single answer. But at the end the poet finds himself able to assert the value and the satisfaction of his vocation as a poet, despite the hostility of the times to the values he holds dear. Do you find this convincing? I do, although I sense something near to desperation in the final assertions.

Now read the next poem, 'Nineteen Hundred and Nineteen', and formulate your general impressions of it. Do you see any significant relationship between it and the 'Meditations'?

DISCUSSION

'Nineteen Hundred and Nineteen' was written four years earlier, as its title indicates, during the war which followed the declaration of the Dublin Dail in January that Ireland had seceded from the United Kingdom. I think you will agree that it is a far more bitter poem than 'Meditations'. It is evident that the war came to Yeats as conclusive and distressing evidence of the failure of the generally optimistic 'progressive' civilisation of the early century. (For many Englishmen the Great War of 1914-18 was evidence of the same failure.)

Section I – again in dignified eight-line rhyming stanzas – tells of the destruction of civilisation; it is a lament. But surprisingly the focus is not yet on Ireland, but on Greece: what have gone are the works of the Athenian sculptor Phidias (ᶜ490-ᶜ450 BC), the grasshopper brooches mentioned by the historian Thucydides in the *History of the Peloponnesian War* (I, 6), and – the 'ancient image made of olive wood' – the statue of Athena Polias in the Erechtheum on the Acropolis at Athens. These artefacts are then referred to ironically as 'pretty toys' and compared to the naive beliefs of the previous decades – confidence in the objectivity of the law, optimism about the power and value of public opinion, and the progressive improvement of mankind. In those days – the Edwardian period – people thought of armies as necessary only for ceremonial purposes. Now things are appallingly different, as the fourth stanza powerfully shows. Violence is destroying the innocent, unpunished; the hope of a peaceful future was an empty dream because, the final image of the weasels suggests, men are only violent animals.

Nevertheless, as we have often seen in other poems, the poet does not readily surrender to total pessimism. He sees one comfort: that 'triumph' – the creation of a successful civilisation – would 'break upon his ghostly solitude'. The solitude of the spirit, so highly valued, would be diluted. However, the doubts go deeper, and another problem is raised. Since 'man is in love, and loves what vanishes', there is nothing more to be said. (Note, in passing, how the use of the question form in the poem gives a dramatic force lacking in this paraphrase.) No-one would previously have admitted how destructive humanity is, though human history from Greece to Ireland – and beyond – is littered with the appalling evidence. Perhaps, though, now the thought is being admitted, humanity can do something about it? That idea is no doubt part of my wishful thinking; there is no hint in the poem that Yeats sees such a comforting possibility.

The second section briefly brings to life a scene danced by the American dancer Loie Fuller (1862-1928) and her (actually Japanese) troupe, which Yeats had seen. It emblematises the idea of humanity being 'whirled . . . round' in a path chosen for it by a more powerful force. This is then compared to the Platonic Year, the 2000-year phase of history seen in *A Vision* as the period in which a civilisation develops and declines. The change from one era to the next is complete, but there is no progress: one form of right and wrong gives way to another. The last two lines bring these ideas together, seeing 'all men' as dancers, participating in the inexorable movement of history. The emphasis on the barbaric nature of the music makes this dance sinister – the positive connotations of the dancer we have found elsewhere are strikingly absent in this evocation of a sense of human powerlessness.

The three stanzas of the third section use the image of the swan to investigate the relation of the individual to history. The swan is seen as a fitting image for 'the solitary soul' because of its pride and power. It is free from the impurity which human activity brings, according to the second stanza. But the flight of the swan, however powerfully imaging the soul's potentiality for the absolute, is disturbing to the living, it 'can bring wildness' and an apocalyptic desire to destroy everything. The temptation of this extremity is related to the failure of the dream of progress, now seen to be that of the 'crack-pated' fool. However, that dream is here treated with a respect not afforded to it in *A Vision* and elsewhere in Yeats. We feel that something valuable has been lost.

The fourth brief section gives forceful expression to total disillusionment with recent history in terms of the disturbingly reductive image of the weasel. It leads fittingly into the powerful mockery of the fifth, whose first three succinct stanzas successfully dismiss all those who has been naively optimistic – the great, wise, and good – and then turns its mocking upon itself to great effect. 'Mock mockers after that': the repetition helps to create an effect of anger and helplessness. For the cynicism which seems an intelligent reaction to the failure of the naive may be itself part of the reason for their failure. When did the cleverly cynical ever help constructively? Perhaps the poet implicates himself in the ciriticism. The 'foul storm' has come indeed. The concluding emphasis on 'we' implicates the whole Irish – and English? – race; all 'Traffic' – the emphasis on this word gives a wonderfully dismissive vigour to the line – 'in mockery'. If naive optimism has failed, so apparently has everything else.

The final section moves into a series of nightmare visions: 'Herodias' daughters have returned again'. Yeats's use of this phrase is explained in his Note to the earlier poem 'The Hosting of the Sidhe' (p. 524), where he writes of 'the [whirling] winds that were called the dance of the daughters of Herodias in the Middle Ages'. (Herodias was the mother of the evil Salomé.) The scene is disconcerting, inexplicable. It culminates in the appearance of Robert Artisson with his 'stupid straw-pale locks'. Yeats's Note tells us that Artisson was 'an evil spirit much run after in Kilkenny at the start of the fourteenth century' (p. 535). Evidently Lady Kyteler was one of his victims, bringing sacrifices to him. What does this strange concluding image singify? To me, primarily the power of evil, drawing humanity into destructive action. The weirdness of the reference opens our responses up, forces us to interpret – but doesn't allow us to do so except in the poem's own grim terms. There is no sign of the reassurance found at the end of 'Meditations' in the poet's insight into these 'daemonic images'. Here the horrors of history overwhelm everything else in a poem fittingly described by Donald Stauffer as 'that most powerfully bitter and desolating of all his poems'.[17]

Looking back on the poem, do you see it as directly related to its predecessors in the volume? And in what ways?

DISCUSSION

I think we can see a continuing concern over transience and the destruction of what is valued. But perhaps there is a stronger sense here, especially in the free use of the plural 'We', of the poet's being totally implicated in the shared human experience which constitutes history.

Following 'Nineteen Hundred and Nineteen', the reader finds himself — or herself — confronted with a number of shorter, apparently simpler poems, beginning with 'The Wheel' and 'Youth and Age'. It is a suitable point at which to pause and look back at the four important meditative poems. How much do they have in common? Are we aware of a single developing argument? What is the effect of Yeats's having decided to print them in an order which, as the given dates show, is anti-chronological?

DISCUSSION

These are large questions, and answers to them will no doubt vary. To take the last question first, it seems to me that the anti-chronological ordering has an effect of reducing possible complacency. 'Nineteen Hundred and Nineteen' is the grimmest of the group, the only one that ends with no effect of resolution but with the disturbing vision of the 'insolent fiend Robert Artisson'. To have opened with it and then moved through to 'Sailing to Byzantium' would perhaps have suggested a too-easy process of coming to terms with the situations considered — those of warring Ireland and the ageing poet. Perhaps, too, Yeats wanted to open with a poem that is clearly not limited in scope to Irish concerns: no doubt he was aware of the possibility of being seen by English reviewers as a limitedly Irish poet. Not that the volume can be said to avoid the Irish situation; we have already seen how central it is. But Yeats can be seen as dealing with it in the context of a broad philosophical understanding, not parochially.

Common concerns? Yes, certainly: old age and the condition of Ireland. Do you see these as totally separate themes? We might see them as related in the fact that both imply longing for some kind of stability amid the flux of human history. But I think it is evident that even living in a just society would by no means compensate the poet for his knowledge of age. That can only be answered by the power of the imagination, or by a kind of abstraction offered by the tradition of Plato and Plotinus, but here rejected as inhuman.

A single developing argument? My impression is that this is not what we experience. There is rather a series of encounters between the poet's mind and these recurring questions, in which he tries to find grounds on which the authority of the imagination can be asserted. But because the imagination is necessarily pulled into the world of the senses, the world of flux, that authority is hard to establish. Nevertheless, it is the poetry's continuing concern.

Now read through the rest of the poems in the volume. What do you notice about them by comparison?

DISCUSSION

A difference of scale. After the four substantial poems we have discussed, we find sixteen others (one of which contains eleven sections) in twenty-three pages. Does this suggest any modification of Kenner's argument about the unity of *The Tower*?

Not necessarily, but I think in fact the reader is likely to feel that these poems, though linking with each other in various ways, usually thematically or in imagery, are more various and hetero-geneous than those so far looked at. The short poems often give the impression of being vivid responses to particular preoccupations. They are none the less striking for that.

The first two, 'The Wheel' and 'Youth and Age', are epigrammatical and thus simplified comments on themes we have become familiar with. Their succinctness and the effect of the rhyme make them vigorous assertions of a grim view respectively of life (with undertones of the Freudian death-wish) and of worldly success.

'The New Faces' is a more dignified, elegiac poem, which reverts to the longer ten-syllable line. The tone is elevated, the diction traditional: the unusual but botanically accurate 'catalpa tree' in conjunction with 'scented lime' gives an effect of splendour, but under the cloud of the opening line's reference to age and death. The poem is addressed to a colleague – one with whom the poet has produced work 'that shall break the teeth of Time' – dramatic hyperbole indeed! We may assume that this is Lady Gregory, and the world invoked is that of the great house of the opening of 'Meditations . . .'. But the point here is to affirm: the poet would not revisit the house if she were to die first. He would not need to do so, because their presence remains in the house, making the living 'more shadowy' than their spiritual predecessors. In this view, 'the new faces' can never replace the old who have won a kind of immortality, we may assume, by the value of what has been achieved in that place. Here we have another kind of victory over time.

'A Prayer for My Son', by contrast, admits with moving humanity, the fragility of life. In the previous volume, 'Michael Robartes and the Dancer' (1919), Yeats had published the splendid 'A Prayer for My Daughter', with its meditation on the significance of custom and ceremony (see *Collected Poems*, pp. 211–14). The poem for Michael, the second-born, is much simpler and gentler. The four stanzas take the form of a prayer, and the poem employs more Christian references than is common in Yeats. The first stanza calls on a 'strong ghost' or guardian angel to protect the sleeping child, and so – more unusually perhaps in a poem written by a man – enable the mother to have her necessary 'fill of sleep'. The second stanza is grander in its claims, expressing concern over the 'devilish' hostility of the world to cultural values – 'the bays'. The third stanza directly addresses Jesus as the God who was once a human child, and is therefore by implication particularly well suited to the protection of a young boy. The fourth invokes the biblical story of the flight of Joseph and Mary with the baby Jesus to Egypt to avoid Herod's persecution. The stanza is a single sentence, the last four lines giving the effect of the hurry to escape, but ending with the emphasis on 'human love'. Even God depended on such protection. I find it interesting that in a poem employing a central Christian story, the emphasis actually moves away from the 'strong ghost', the supernatural presence, to finally come to rest on 'human love'. Yeats's feelings about his baby son have produced a poem which stands out in its tenderness.

The next poem, as Yeats's Note (p. 535) tells us, consists of two songs sung by the Musicians in his play *The Resurrection*. (See *Collected Plays*, pp. 579–594.) The title shows that Yeats had been paying particular attention at this time to Christian ideas. (The play itself, incidentally, is well worth reading.) The poem opens with a vivid account of the Greek myth concerning the death of the god Dionysus, whose heart is saved by Athena, so making his resurrection possible. Here the story is linked to the 'Magnus Annus', the Great – or Platonic – Year referred to in the second section of 'Nineteen Hundred and Nineteen'; another cycle of history is beginning, that of 'Another Troy . . . Another Argo . . .'. But where are we, historically? When did the Roman Empire stand 'appalled'? At the time, referred to in the previous poem, of the birth of Christ. The poem is concerned with the end of the Greek cycle, and the beginning of the Christian. The fourth *Eclogue* of the Roman poet Virgil had given an account of the ending of the Golden Age, when the goddess of justice, Astrea, had left the earth to be transformed into the constellation Virgo. From the time of the Council of Nicea (325 AD) onwards, Christians had interpreted the

Ecologue as a prophecy of the birth of Christ, Astrea being equated with the Virgin Mary, and the prominent star Spica in the constellation Virgo with the Star of Bethlehem.

The second Song thus begins with an account of the conflict between Christianity and Hellenism. The phrase 'a fabulous and formless darkness' had been used by E. R. Dodds in *Select Passages Illustrating Neo-Platonism* (1923), paraphrasing an ancient account of that conflict, and describing the Christian Church as seen by Hellenism. All the restraints of Greek civilisation are shown giving way to the intense irrationality of the new epoch: Yeats, as you can see, was fond of vivid simplificatory myths of history! The last stanza is more general, affirming both the creative and the destructive power of humanity. Nothing lasts, everything has its origin in man's 'resinous heart'. This is a very striking image. It is from man's heart that comes the power to feed the 'flames' – a word effectively including both creative and destructive implications. But the application of the adjective to the heart itself emphasises the dangers of the creative power. So we have a fine balance, in this final assertion – like that in 'Meditations', between these two elements. The sweep of the rhythm makes it sound positive, but beneath lurks the disturbing recognition of the destructive power of time.

'Fragments' consists of two linked assertions, and was added in 1931. Why do you think Yeats thought it appropriate here?

Perhaps because of the view of history and the assertion that truth is derived not from the empirical tradition of Locke (English, and associated with the Industrial Revolution) but from the revelations of the spirit, such as those Yeats had received from the spirit-writings of his wife. As in the 'Two Songs', Yeats is looking to myth for revelation. This is true also of the next poem.

'Leda and the Swan' seems to me a particularly powerful and disturbing poem. Why do you think Yeats chose this subject? (It is one that has figured prominently in Western art, including the painting 'Leda' by the late nineteenth-century French artist Gustave Moreau which Yeats knew; the critic Giorgio Melchiori has discussed the sources of this poem in great detail.[18]) How do you respond to the subject-matter and tone of the poem? What is your understanding of the last line? Do women readers feel that the poem embodies a male insensitivity to female vulnerability?

DISCUSSION

Whatever your final view, I think you will agree that the poem dramatises with great force the classical story that Zeus came to

Leda in the form of a swan, and that from their union of the divine and human was born Helen of Troy – so often associated in Yeats's mind with Maud Gonne. (The story also includes the birth of Polydeuces, and sometimes of Castor too, but they are not relevant to the poem.)

For someone like Yeats who wanted to believe in the interpenetration of the divine and the human the story had an obvious appeal. And in view of the references in related poems, we can see it as part of a series of unorthodox meditations on the idea of incarnation, which is central to Christianity.

The poem's power owes much to its compression: the first three words take us into the action with no time for a complete grammatical sentence. The concentrated fourteen-line form of the sonnet has seldom had more packed into it than here. We are scarcely aware of the tight rhyme scheme – look down the line-endings to check the tightness – which helps to create the appropriate sense of controlled force. The poem is set out on the page in a way that emphasises its four sections, but the progression is far from orderly and no neat conclusion is reached. The first two quatrains dramatise the rape itself, and in stark physical terms which stress the woman's helplessness to resist the 'white rush' of the swan-god. But the second question suggests something more intimate and mysterious than mere physical intimacy in the beating of the 'strange heart' as felt by Leda. The next two-and-a-half lines neatly summarise the historical results of the rape in the destruction of Troy because of Helen, drawing elegiac power from the the impressive sound as well as the relevant reference, of the name Agamemnon. Think how much less effective Hector or Achilles would have sounded! But it is the final question, covering the last three-and-a-half lines, which is the intellectual focus of the poem; and by far the most difficult section. The reader is reminded of the physical situation already evoked, but this time we are asked to try to understand what might have happened within the mind of Leda at that moment. She was 'mastered', experiencing the 'power' of the male god; did she share 'his knowledge' while the intimacy lasted? I think the implied answer is 'yes', and the suggestion that for a moment Leda shared the god's knowledge of all the historical implications of the event. Humanity is passive in the grip of historical forces, but it may glimpse the significance of what is happening. The poem itself is a glimpse of that significance.

This one of a small number of poems of which Yeats himself discussed the origins. In a note in 1924, he explained:

> I wrote Leda and the Swan because the editor of a political review
> asked me for a poem . . . My fancy began to play with Leda and the

Swan for metaphor [for 'some movement from above preceded by
some violent annunciation'], and I began this poem; but as I wrote,
bird and lady took such possession of the scene that all politics went
out of it, and my friend tells me that his 'conservative readers would
misunderstand the poem'.[19]

(The friend was George Russell, who had become editor of the *Irish
Statesman* in 1923.) This strikes me as very interesting for the light
it throws on the working of the poet's mind. Conscious intention
finds itself drastically modified by imaginative involvement. We are
certainly led firstly to experience the scene itself in all its
physicality, but the conclusion remains to relate the scene to the
wider questions of the kind raised in the previous poems about the
changing cycles of human history.

As to the question whether women readers find the poem's
attitude distasteful, a male view must be irrelevant. But I feel that
the writing does not endorse the 'male' violence which it certainly
evokes.

How does the next poem relate to others in the volume?

DISCUSSION

The title 'On a picture of a Black Centaur by Edmund Dulac' is
explicit in drawing our attention to Yeats's interest in pictorial art.
Edmund Dulac (1882–1953) was a friend of Yeats, who helped
with the staging of some of his plays.[20] The Black Centaur derives
from Greek mythology, in which we encounter this creature whose
upper part is human, and lower part horse-like, suggesting the
necessary connection between the human and the animal. It is a
difficult poem, it seems to me, as Yeats attempts to interpret
Dulac's visual imagery for his own purposes. The scene evoked is
vivid and strange, a world of stamping hooves and 'horrible green
parrots'. At first only the murderousness of that world is
emphasised. Then the poet gives an account of his own involvement
with 'old mummy wheat'. We no doubt think of the grains of wheat
found in Egyptian tombs which are said to have retained their
powers of growth over the centuries. The poet had toiled to
produce life out of this dead matter, presumably without success;
'but now' he has discovered an equivalent kind of vitality lasting
from the past, imaged in the act of bringing 'full-flavoured wine'
out of a barrel. This is associated with the story of the Seven
Sleepers of Ephesus, believed to have survived persecution by being
immured in a cave for two hundred years. Yeats presents these
Christian martyrs comically as 'seven Ephesian topers', attribu-

ting their sleep' to alcohol rather than spirituality; but he is also celebrating his own discovery of the possibility of bringing truths out of what had once seemed the dead past.

The last quatrain is difficult because it is not obvious to whom it is being addressed. When we go back to the beginning of the poem, we see that it must be the Black Centaur itself. It is invited to sleep 'a long Saturnian sleep' – Saturn ruled in the Golden Age and the phrase suggests contentment. Then the poet admits that he has always loved the Centaur – perhaps a symbol of the imagination, halfway between two worlds? – better than his own soul. The poet is now prepared to take on a protective function towards the Centaur, keeping watch against 'those horrible green birds'. (May those nightmarish creatures be related to the horrific 'brazen hawks' of the 'Meditations'?) The poem seems to be asserting, if not very cogently, that wisdom is to be found not in the 'mad abstract dark' but in the world of conflict inhabited by the Centaur.

If this is so, it provides a thematic link with the next poem, 'Among School Children', which we have already considered as a superb expression of one response to the problem of the transience of human life. I wonder whether reading the poem again now strikes you as in any way a different experience?

I don't think the experience is remarkably different. It is true that we now recognise a number of allusions – to Leda through the 'Ledean body' of the young Maud, to Plato, to the painting of the quattrocento – but the main effect is surely to emphasise the powerful originality of the poem, the sense that it is enacting a newly-minted answer to the problem which re-echoes throughout the volume. If we felt in poems like 'The Tower' that the elements of autobiography were at times at a tangent to the poem's central concerns, here everything is integrated into a powerful unity. The perspective of mother and child enables the poem to achieve an encompassing humanity.

The next poem is a translation of one of the choruses in Sophocles' play *Oedipus at Colonus*. It is not surprising that Yeats, so sharply aware of his own advancing age as well as consistently interested in the theatre, should have developed a particular interest in Sophocles' Oedipus plays, some of the greatest ever written, at this period. Although he did not know Greek, he created a version for the Abbey Theatre, which was successfully produced in 1927, (see *Collected Plays*, pp. 521–575). Here, however, the poem must be considered in its context. It evokes in strongly positive terms the world of Colonus.

What does this poem share with 'Among School Children'? Surely its mood of celebration. The first stanza chooses for celebration in particular the horses, the 'intricacies' of the wood, the nightingale, and above all the strange region amid the sacred wood where a beautiful supernatural dance takes place of 'immortal ladies', companioned gaily by 'Semele's lad', the god Dionysus. The way of describing him humanises the situation by its casualness. The second stanza takes us to the heart of Athenian civilization, the Academy on the outskirts of Athens adjoining Colonus, founded by Plato in ᶜ385 B.C. The 'grey-leaved olive-tree' was valued as the gift of the goddess Athena to mankind; an olive was believed to have sprung up at the Academy first after the primal olive. The poetry confidently asserts the indestructibility of 'that old marvel', watched over by the protective goddess. (Thinking back to Section I of 'Nineteen Hundred and Nineteen' we realise that Hellenic civilisation was not as exempt as it believed from the destructive power of history.) The third stanza continues the celebration by emphasising the natural beauty of the country which affects even the goddess Demeter, whose daughter Persephone was carried off to Hades by the dark god Pluto; the loveliness of the spectacle – Yeats is not afraid to use obviously romantic phraseology – is completed by the river, 'abounding Cephisus'; the adjective services to give an attractive energy to the beautiful scene. The final stanza celebrates the piety of the people of Colonus, who remember the value of the gifts given to them by their god Poseidon, god of the sea and of horses, who taught mankind both to ride and to row: the final image of the 'white horses' neatly brings together the two areas of Poseidon's concern. The poem is one of the few in the volume which maintains a single line of argument throughout: 'Colonus' Praise' is consistently positive and celebratory, sustaining the final note of 'Among School Children'.

I leave you to see if you discern any links to the next poem.

'Wisdom' takes us from Greek to Christian culture, and gives a heterodox view of the discovery of the 'true faith'. This is attributed to Byzantine Christianity, which replaced the accounts of the writers of the four Gospels – each dismissively described as 'some peasant gospeller' – with the splendid imagery of its own artistic vision. Again the tone of the verse is celebratory as we are reminded of the splendours of the pictorial representations of the Divine in Eastern Christianity, which ignores realism to make Mary 'majestic' and to set Jesus among 'stormy towers of Babylon' unreached by the Flood – amusingly described as 'Noah's freshet'. The whole Byzantine account is allegorical: Joseph, Mary and Jesus become Abundance, Innocence and Wisdom. Finally, the 'cognomen' Wisdom is adjudged to be most appropriate, for the paradoxical reason that it took 'wild infancy' to bring serenity to the mother: Wisdom involved recognising that 'wildness' might be necessary to fight the horrors of the world.

It is followed by the equally lively but very different 'The Fool by the Roadside' (a reduced version of the original 'The Hero, the Girl and the Fool'). Here we have a figure from Irish mythology – we may be reminded of the plays of J. M. Synge which Yeats greatly admired. The Fool is contemplating the ending of his life, his thoughts becoming increasingly disorganised like 'loose thread'. As he does so, there drifts into his mind the comforting – and strange – thought that at the stage when he is 'mere shade at last' he may eventually find 'a faithful love' – the repetition of the phrase adds poignancy to the hope. Faithful love is, by implication, not a normal human experience; perhaps it will occur to compensate our spirits after death. Or is the thought more ironical? – that fidelity is likely to occur only when it is neither needed nor valued. The basic feeling of the poem is wistful, by contrast with its predecesors.

'Owen Aherne and his Dancers' develops the reference to love at the end of the Fool's song.[21] Indeed, the colloquial feeling of the verse movement, with its distinctively Irish flavour – 'A strange thing surely . . .' – gives Aherne an immediate presence as he puzzles over the fact that his heart has been driven mad by the burden of unsought love. The Heart has been unable to cope with 'all the tempest' of powerful feelings, imaged in the wind, which accompany love, and has found its refuge in madness. The third stanza completes the story. Aherne is a divided man, partly sane, but forced to leave his love because of the intensity of the emotions aroused in his Heart. The 'I' has been unable to control the Heart.

The second Section brings the Heart into the poem as a speaking voice. It is laughing 'behind its ribs' (giving a physicality to what seemed an allegorical voice), and produces a perfectly logical argument: it has been called 'mad' simply because it has warned the ageing poet against involvement with 'that young child', who was 'so wildly bred'. Like should mate with like. Now we reassess the idea of madness. Perhaps it was the 'I' that wanted to deceive itself? The 'I' then replies, accusing the Heart of lying, denying that he found 'the woman at my side' in any cage, though admitting that she would be upset to learn how far away his thoughts now are from her. The Heart is given the last, effective stanza. It is not bothered what 'I' may say now, so long as the young woman – 'the child' – is left free, not forced by her feelings of gratitude to a man long known to commit herself fully to him. The last line is joyful with the kind of Irish lilt we noted at the opening of the poem, and which is sustained throughout: 'O let her choose a young man now and all for his wild sake'. The Heart, far from being revealed as mad, surely has the better of the argument. It certainly expresses what seems to the reader the 'natural' view about marriage partners, and deploys the adjective 'wild' at the end in a characteristically Yeatsian way; it suggests here the energy and freedom that ought to be a part of youthful experience, and which in no sense characterise Owen Aherne.

For of course Owen Aherne sounds very like Yeats, and we realise that the poem can be interpreted in direct biographical terms. It was in Normandy that Yeats had proposed to Iseult Gonne, and been rejected. This poem enacts Yeats's divided response to that event. Do you feel that it belongs more to Yeats's life than to the poetic context?

I'm not sure. Every effort has certainly been made to 'depersonalise' the poem. Perhaps it is our reading which ought to be criticised if it puts this poem into a separate category. Here it is integrated into a sequence, leading into the series of meditations entitled 'A Man Young and Old' which clearly relates to it but generalises its concerns further.

Now read the sequence. What account does it give of love? How do the experiences of the young and the old man differ? Why does the sequence end with the Oedipus poem?

DISCUSSION

These are compressed and often cryptic poems, but I think you will agree that the main feeling which they convey is of the inadequacy and pain of human love. In this, the experiences of the old man – reached by poem VI – are not markedly different from those of the young man in the early poems which take place in a landscape dominated by the female and destructive image of the moon. The strongest feelings are of suffering, whether in the 'maundering' lover of I, transformed into a 'lout'; the stony lover of II achieving dignity in dumbness; the 'swimming lad' drowned by the 'cruel happiness' of the mermaid in III; the contemplation of death in IV linked to the loss of the beloved's 'wildness'; or the cup of V, with its sexual connotations, equally unsatisfying when full and when empty. In the poems associated with the old man there is a paradoxical vitality, with the extraordinary claim in VI that Helen had once taken pleasure with the man, the assertion in VII that 'Laughter not time destroyed my voice', the positive conclusion of VIII with its imagery of bursting and blossoming (though that is firmly set in the past); the relish taken in the stories of the old in IX, and even in X the lyrical energy of the opening suggesting the power of the imagination to carry one beyond life – though the final lines assert (with their reference back to 'old Madge' of VII) the impossibility of forgetting the human world.

In this context, the sombre advice of the final great Chorus in *Oedipus at Colonus*, addressed to the 'travel-wearied aged man' as he approaches death, seems highly appropriate. The delights of the world – even those celebrated earlier in 'Colonus' Praise' – are now seen to lead only to tragic entanglements. Humanity continues to celebrate with 'laughing dancers', but the old who are aware of the full truth can celebrate only the ending of life. It is best not to live at all; next best is 'a gay goodnight and quickly turn away' – early death. For Oedipus, for the old man who has narrated these poems, for the ageing Yeats, there is no comfort to be found, at least not in the central experience of human life, love. The sequence ends with sombre power.

This sequence of poems is followed, rather surprisingly, by a brief, ironic, public poem about the statues which then stood in O'Connell Street in Dublin: those of Horatio Nelson – the tallest – and the Irish leaders Daniel O'Connell and Charles Stewart Parnell. It was a favourite place for public meetings, and Yeats takes occasion to mock the 'popular statesmen' – for him, a contradiction in terms – who base all their rhetoric on the ideal of purity. We are suddenly taken back into Yeats's involvement with political controversies at the time, and his feeling that Ireland was falling into the hands of a narrow-minded and self-righteous Catholic Nationalism. These 'statesmen' cling to the idea of purity, setting it in opposition to 'base ambition' and the dangers of pride of intellect. By implication, they are content to be complacently unintelligent and unadventurous. It is the last line which brings the poem to life. The 'three old rascals', as they are familiarly called, 'laugh aloud'. They know that political life must be conducted intelligently – and often deviously – and that ambition is a necessary basis for political achievement. Their laughter is an ironic comment on the pomposity and hypocrisy of their successors. It concludes an entertaining poem which brings us from more general themes into contemporary Dublin.

But we do not stay there. Originally, as we have seen, 'The Three Monuments' was followed by the seven-page narrative poem 'The Gift of Harun Al-Rashid', in which the Arabian setting distances an autobiographical account of Yeats's wife Georgie as a spirit-medium. Yeats obviously decided that the length of the poem was excessive in its context and so concluded with 'All Souls' Night', already discussed, in which the Oxford setting soon gives

place to a meditation on the 'marvellous thing' which the spirit of
Yeats has discovered, the 'mummy truths' which outlive the
changing civilisations of Greece, Italy or Ireland.

Does it change your experience of 'All Souls' Night' to come to
it as the conclusion to the whole volume?

It seems to me that the poem gains a good deal by being seen as
the culmination of a series of meditations on the problems of
human life, and in particular those of love. If, as the *Oedipus* poem
suggested, 'Never to have lived is best', then only the supernatural
can offer any consolation for, or escape from, the problems and
sufferings of humanity. And this is what 'All Souls' Night' asserts.
There is a sense of conclusiveness about it: though in Yeats, we
come to learn, any firm conclusion may develop into a stage of the
next evolving argument.

Now read 'The Gift of Harun Al-Rashid' (pp. 513–19). Does it
reveal the same concerns as the other poems we have been reading?
Do you think Yeats was right to omit it from *The Tower*?

DISCUSSION

I think we can see that it does share both autobiographical and
thematic material. We cannot fail to see the closeness of Yeats to
the Court philosopher in the poem, Kusta ben Luka, who has been
given by 'the great Harun Al-Rashid' (an eighth-century Caliph of
Baghdad discussed in *A Vision*[22]) a young wife who turns out to be
a medium. The truths revealed through her mediumship, however
abstract in the forms given to them by Kusta, are 'but a new
expression of her body/Drunk with the bitter sweetness of her
youth'. Wisdom, it would seem, can be revealed only to the man
who can stand close to the 'storm-tossed banner' of a woman's
beauty without losing his self-possession. To him 'the armed man
speaks' – perhaps in tones similar to those in which the Swan
'spoke' to Leda. Wisdom, insight, life, stand in complex relationships. Old wisdom comes through the young woman. The Caliph
may be generous, but he belongs to the world of nature ('Every day
I ride with falcon to the river's edge,/Or carry the ringed mail upon
my back,/Or court a woman'). Kusta ben Luka, like Yeats, wants to
'hear the armed man speak' a wisdom beyond nature, though
communicable only with its imagery. (Incidentally, whether or not
the volume would gain by the inclusion of this poem, there seems to
me no doubt that it gains by being read within the volume.)

This brings us to the question of Yeats's decision to omit the
poem. What is your view? I think that on the whole his judgment
was correct; the length of the poem, its leisurely narrative mode in

blank verse, would be difficult to integrate with a reading of the more succinct lyrics. But we have seen that it is closely connected with such poems as 'Fragments' and 'All Souls' Night'. Its inclusion would have strengthened the autobiographical element in the volume, in its moving expression gratitude to the young medium-woman whose revelations mean so much to the Yeatsian persona.

What is the effect of reading the volume in the way suggested by Kenner's argument, which we have been following in our discussions?

I believe that to read *The Tower* as a sequence of linked meditations on related themes is to find the individual poems, many of them very impressive in themselves, further enriched. For we have a stronger sense of the vitality of the poet's mind as it engages with important themes and ironies. Denis Donoghue, whose brief book on Yeats' is brilliantly illuminating, suggests that we should see the arrangement of the *Collected Poems* as 'a kind of play'[23], though he warns that any simple idea of evolutionary development is irrelevant:

> The idiom of development is misleading, it implies evolution. The relation between *The Tower* and the major books before and after, *Michael Robartes and the Dancer* and *The Winding Stair and Other Poems*, is a dialectical relation, and we do well to think of the books as personalities in a play.[24]

This strikes me as a valuable suggestion.

If we accept the analogy, we may now feel in a position to say something about the 'personality' of *The Tower*. Donoghue's own remarks about that volume are striking and convincing. He suggests that the poetry is sustained in excitement by its dialectical quality, and that one of the aspects of that dialectic is that between Symbol – the construction of the human imagination – and History – 'whatever the imagination recognises as distinct from itself.' For Donoghue, '*The Wild Swans at Coole* is history, consistent with symbolism; *The Tower* is symbolism, glancing ruefully at history.'

I think you will see the suggestiveness of this if you think back over the poems we have been considering. In *The Tower* Yeats was seeking an elevation from which the bloody experience of history might be contemplated without distress. In 'All Souls' Night' such a security has been found. But we do not have a sense of simple progress towards a solution, but rather of the increasing complexity of the problem for which the final solution offered may actually seem too simple. However, I think you can see the sense in which *The Tower* 'is symbolism'. As we move on to the following volume we will want to bear in mind this description, and the general idea of the balance between symbol and history, and to attempt our definition of that volume's 'personality' in its contribution to the overall 'play' of the *Collected Poems*.

4   The Winding Stair

By the time *The Tower* was published in February 1928, Yeats was in Italy, at Rapallo, recovering from illness and well looked after by his protective wife. His letters – published in a fine edition by Allan Wade in 1954[1] – cast a good deal of light on the period, and are full of interest. Many of them are to his old friend Olivia Shakespeare, whose daughter had married Ezra Pound, now living at Rapallo; these are particularly affectionate and intelligent, and tell us much about his changing attitudes and concerns. They also show an affection for his young children which does not often find expression in the poetry. When *The Tower* appeared, Yeats was struck by its bitterness, for him very much part of having lived through the Irish situation of those years. He told Mrs Shakespeare, 'Re-reading *The Tower* I was astonished at its bitterness, and long to live out of Ireland that I may find some new vintage'[2] – though he also feared that without the bitterness his poetry might become weaker. But his mood now was less bitter, as comes out in his observation to Lady Gregory: '*Tower* is receiving great favour. Perhaps the reviewers know that [I] am ill, and think that I am so ill that I can be recommended without future inconvenience'.[3] He had previously told her of Rapallo, 'This is an indescribably lovely place. . . . Here I shall put off the bitterness of Irish quarrels, and write my most amiable verses'.[4] We shall see whether we find the new volume more 'amiable'.

The *Winding Stair* as we now read it is a bringing together of two volumes. *The Winding Stair* as it first appeared from the Fountain Press in New York in October 1929 was a small volume,

consisting only of the first five poems as we now have them, from
'In Memory . . .' to 'Oil and Blood', together with the eleven poems
of the sequence 'A Woman Young and Old', now placed at the very
end of the volume. Yeats was prompted to produce this volume so
rapidly by an offer of £300 from William Rudge of the Fountain
Press in September 1927. He had already written the 'Woman
Young and Old' poems, and now set about adding to them. He
wrote to Mrs Shakespeare in October:

> I am giving him 'The Woman Young and Old', a poem called 'Blood
> and the Moon' (a Tower poem) which was written weeks ago, and I
> am writing a new tower poem 'Sword and Tower' [later, 'A Dialogue
> of Self and Soul'], which is a choice of rebirth rather than deliverance
> from birth. I make my Japanese sword and its silk covering my
> symbol of life.[5]

The reference to two of these as *Tower* poems might suggest that
the new volume would not be marking totally new preoccupations
from its predecessor, or at least that the first group of poems in it
would not.

　　The second volume of relevant poems was *Words for Music
Perhaps and Other Poems*, published by the Cuala Press in Dublin
in November 1932. This opened with 'Byzantium', and contained
all the rest of the poems now found under the heading *The Winding
Stair* in the *Collected Poems*, concluding with the sequence 'Words
for Music Perhaps'. The two poems then entitled 'Meditation upon
Death at Algeciras' and 'Mohini Chatterjee' had already appeared
under the title 'Meditations upon Death' in *A Packet for Ezra
Pound* in August 1929 – a strange book in which Yeats tried to
explain his philosophy to his old friend, also criticising Pound's
own outlook severely. The writing of these poems took place
between February 1929 and May 1932, when Lady Gregory,
whom Yeats had been staying with at Coole in her final illness,
died. The 'Words for Music Perhaps' group – the title offering
lyricism and then withholding it – was mostly written quickly at
Rapallo. Yeats was surprised by the speed of his writing, and even
worried as to whether it was not too easy. He told Mrs Shakespeare,
'I have written eleven lyrics in the last two months – nine of them
Words for Music, these last unlike my past work – wilder and
perhaps slighter'.[6] He sent her 'Lullaby' (pp. 300–1), and later the
more personal 'Speech after long silence.'[7] Immediately after this he
fell ill with Maltese fever, not recovering until March 1930. The
letters say less about the later poems in the volume, except for a
draft of 'Vacillation' VII (p. 285) which Yeats sent to Mrs
Shakespeare on 3 Jan 1932 with an interesting commentary:

I feel that this is the choice of the Saint (St Theresa's ecstasy, Gandhi's smiling face): Comedy; and the Heroic choice: Tragedy (Dante, Don Quixote). Live tragically but be not deceived (not the fool's Tragedy).[8]

There is an agreeable irony in the note on the back of the envelope referring to the last line of the poem: 'Leave the 'And' out of the last line of the poem. Have vacillated all day. Not 'And what sang' but 'What sang?' ' The vacillations were not exclusively philosophical.

When the composite volume with which we are concerned was about to appear, in August 1933, the Crazy Jane poems and the following love poems were again those to which he referred. He describes them as 'exciting and strange. Sexual abstinence fed their fire – I was ill and yet full of desire. They sometimes came out of the greatest mortal excitement I am capable of'.[9] The writing of these poems had clearly been an unusual and exciting experience for him. Whether it is equally exciting for the reader we shall consider later. But it is worth emphasising that the volume contains many other poems to which Yeats drew no special attention. His most interesting self-critical remarks at this time did not in fact refer to the volume we are considering, but to his work as a whole. Macmillans were now preparing an edition of Yeats's *Collected Poems*, which was to appear in New York and London in November 1933. Yeats was correcting the proofs in the previous year, when he wrote to Mrs Shakespeare:

> '[I] am greatly astonished at myself . . . I keep saying what man is this who . . . says the same thing in so many different ways . . . My first denunciation of old age I made in *The Wanderings of Usheen* (end of part 1) before I was twenty and the same denunciation comes in the last pages of the book. The swordsman throughout repudiates the saint, but not without vacillation. Is that perhaps the whole theme – Usheen and Patrick – 'so get you gone Von Hügel though with blessings on your head'?[10]

This last is a quotation from the final section of 'Vacillation' (p. 286).

As we now move to read the poems in the volume, we can test out the helpfulness of Yeats's suggestion. Bearing in mind his suggested antithesis of Swordsman – the man of action – and Saint – the man of contemplation – we can attend to the poems as we encounter them – though we may feel that the exclusively masculine terminology of this antithesis may leave some gaps or problems in a volume where, from a mere reading of the titles, women's presence is strongly felt. We may also wish to ponder the implications of the volume's title, which is the more deliberate for not being that of any specific poem.

Now read through the volume, noting any continuities of setting or theme which strike you. Do you think it possesses the same kind of unity as *The Tower*?

My view – influenced no doubt to some extent by my knowledge of the publishing history – is that it is rather more heterogeneous, but that there is one central preoccupation: with the question of how humanity is to respond to knowledge of the inevitability of death. But in offering his responses to this question, Yeats shows extraordinary vitality and variety of resource.

Let us now work our way through a number of individual poems.

Unlike *The Tower*, *The Winding Stair* begins with one of its less ambitious poems, 'In Memory of Eva Gore-Booth and Con Markiewicz'. The elegiac note will be heard frequently in the volume, as Yeats continues to be concerned with his own ageing, but often measure this in relation to others. Here the poem's eight-syllable lines flow colloquially, the relaxed effect supported by the use of half – rather than full – rhymes (south, both; wreath, death; ignorant, gaunt . . .). The opening four lines vividly create a recollected scene with the two young women, the sisters Eva and Constance Gore-Booth. Yeats had known the sisters at their country house, Lissadell in County Sligo, in the 1890s. The poem repeats the memory of the two beautiful girls in their 'silk kimonos', one 'a gazelle' – the shy elegant creature embodies everything that age has destroyed in the two women. The tone of the second section opens in an affectionate address to the dead women – Eva had died in 1926 and Constance in 1927 – 'Dear shadows, now you know it all'. The poem suggests that they were wrong to concern themselves with political issues – time is the only real enemy of fine people such as they had been. But the ending is not sombre but exuberant. The poet calls on the 'shadows' to help him in setting fire to time to produce a great conflagration. The mood seems celebratory as the poet joins himself with the sisters in the strange assertion: 'We the great gazebo built.' A gazebo is defined in the *Oxford English Dictionary* as 'A turret or lantern on the roof of a house, commanding an extensive prospect; also, a similar erection in a garden'. An eighteenth-century word, it suggests the world of landscape-gardening and elegant follies. The poet seeks to ally himself with the vanished world of the Anglo-Irish Gore-Booths, 'convicted . . . of guilt' by modern Ireland. The gesture the poet wants to make is an apocalyptic one, challenging time in its audacity. It is a long way from the quiet retrospect with which the poem had opened.

It does not seem to me that this poem needs elaborate

annotation for it to make its effect. However, you may like to have
a little more information about the Gore-Booth sisters. Eva wrote
poetry, while Constance, who became by marriage Countess
Markiewicz, participated in the Easter Rising in 1916 (see the –
rather derogatory – account at the beginning of the second section
of the poem, commemorating that event, p. 203.) She was
sentenced to death, but the sentence was commuted; she was
released in the Amnesty of 1917, and was active in Irish left-wing
politics. Note the poet's way of referring to such activities:
'Conspiring among the ignorant'. I leave it to you to decide how far
you share Yeats's view.

Next comes the brief poem 'Death'. Yeats's 1933 letter to
Edmund Dulac, printed as a Note, states:

> I think I was roused to write 'Death' and 'Blood and the Moon' by
> the assassination of Kevin O'Higgins, the finest intellect in Irish
> public life, and, I think I may add, to some extent, my friend. (pp.
> 536–7)

O'Higgins, Vice-President and Minister for Justice, had been
responsible for the severe implementation of laws against the illegal
carrying of arms, which involved the execution of some members of
the IRA; he was shot by unidentified assassins on his way to mass
on 10 July 1927. The poem, however, written in six-syllable lines
rhyming alternately, is assertive but general. The death of animals,
with no sense of the future, is contrasted with that of man,
'Dreading and hoping all'. He has experienced death and survived
many times already in his imagination. The sentence about the
'Great man in his pride/Confronting murderous men' powerfully
evokes an all-too familiar scene from recent history, but once again
the poem emphasises the positive element in the tragedy. 'Supersession of breath' – ambiguous, because supersession can mean either
'The act of superseding or condition of being superseded' – is made
trivial by the pride (always a positive term, as we have seen) of the
great man under attack. 'He knows death to the bone' – the grim
simplicity of this has a positive quality that leads into the assertion
of the last line. Of course the assassins have 'created death' in one
sense; but more significantly 'Man' has done so in his ability –
exemplified at its most impressive for Yeats in great men like
O'Higgins – to see his life as having shape and meaning. Dying
animals, unconscious of death, cannot undergo the same experience
as man. The poem is packed and energetic; but do you find that
Yeats succeeds in integrating the more general argument about
human consciousness with the tribute to O'Higgins?

The poem that follows, 'A Dialogue of Self and Soul',

continues the concern with death, but treats it in the more spacious form of the eight-line stanza. Why do you think the poet chooses this form? How does his choice of it contribute to the overall effect of the poem? Do you consider it important to reflect on such 'technical' details?

DISCUSSION

I hope your answer to the last question was positive. The formal structure of any poem – indeed, of any piece of writing – conditions, even if we do not realise it, our whole reading experience. It is one of the tasks of criticism to try to integrate our responses – or perhaps rather to indicate the ways in which they are integrated for us by the fact that we are reading a particular kind of discourse, poetry. We cannot give a full reading of the poem without making ourselves aware of the effects of formal organisation. The reader of Yeats will immediately recognise in these stanzas, even if the rhyme-scheme is different,[1] a form which he or she will associate with some of the most authoritative poetry of the previous volumes. It seems likely that it was to create this effect of authority that the form was chosen. It helps to give the argument between the Self – the worldly part of humanity – and the Soul – the spiritual aspect – a good deal of weight. The poem is not obscure, and Yeats has a helpful Note (pp. 535–6) discussing his use of traditional symbols in the volume, particularly those of the tower and the gyres (of which the winding or spiral stair is one form).

I suggest you read the Note and the poem, and see how far your account corresponds with the one I am about to give.

DISCUSSION

The poet divides his personality into two aspects, who both attempt to come to terms with the approach of death. The Soul employs imagery of ascent, starting with 'the winding ancient stair' which gives its name to the entire volume. The Soul is out to convert the Self, which it obviously knows to be sensual and worldly, to persuade it (him?) to ascend to the heights of spirituality, which move through the 'starlit air' and 'the star that marks the hidden pole' into total 'darkness'. The rhythm moves smoothly, almost hypnotically, with the repeated use of 'Upon' and the imperative 'set' and 'fix', until we reach the final line with its striking question. The Soul is associated with darkness, mystery, the beyond.

In the second stanza the Self, the worldly part of man, ignores the question and the summons, and seems totally involved in its concentration on 'Sato's ancient blade', the Japanese sword encountered earlier in Part III of 'Meditations . . .'. The movement of the verse is slower; the contemplation of the sword is like a ritual, an effect enhanced by the complicated order of words in the final line, which forces us to read slowly and carefully.

The Soul returns to the attack, seeing the implications of what the Self is contemplating, which it describes as 'Emblematical of love and war'. It reminds the Self of its age, and repeats the advice to think spiritually: 'Think of ancestral night'. If imagination can learn to 'scorn the earth' and intellect to control its wanderings, then night can 'Deliver from the crime of death and birth'. In the night of pure spirit, the cycle of existence is transcended.

However, the Self remains imperturbable – I think we should find a certain amusement in this non-communication. (You will find that Harold Bloom in a discussion of this poem in his lively book on Yeats remarks that the title might well have been 'Two Monologues of Self and Soul'.)[12] Actually the Soul tries hard, and does elicit a response, if a negative one. The Self firstly continues its meditation on the sword, emphasising its age and the beauty of the embroideries in which it is wrapped, but then goes on to see these as 'emblems of the day' against the tower and night of the Soul's allegiance, claiming for itself the right to 'commit the crime' – of participation in life or renewing the life cycle – 'once more'.

By now the Soul has fallen into a kind of trance as it contemplates the idea of ascending to Heaven. In the spiritual condition to which it aspires all the normal human senses become irrelevant and intellect itself can no longer make its necessary distinctions. This is the higher plane where forgiveness can occur – but only for the dead. The ideas which the Soul is trying to express now are so difficult from a human point of view that they cannot be uttered; paradoixically, the tongue of the nearly disembodied Soul becomes a material object, a stone. Perhaps petrifaction is the path to sanctity? At least, the Soul has 'ascended' to a point at which it can no longer participate in the dialogue.

And so the four stanzas of the powerful second part are all uttered by the increasingly triumphant Self. The first two stanzas summarise a life – are a version of autobiography, indeed. But this is introduced by the statement that 'A living man' – by contrast with 'the dead' of whom the Soul has just spoken – 'is blind and drinks his drop'. Again we have a suggestion of the world of Synge, or Beckett, of blindness as metaphor and drunkenness as a human condition. The 'ditches' of experience may be 'impure', but that is inevitable. Life will take disagreeable shape, as it has done in that of the Self as now described. There is no way in which man can escape the effects of 'malicious eyes' upon his own idea of himself: and that the 'defiling and disfigured shape' is not solely to be attributed to the malice of others is suggested by the use of the term 'mirror'. Or if he could escape, it would only be into 'the wintry blast' in which honour would be small comfort.

After this grim summary, we might expect a despairing conclusion. But the opposite happens. Once again the poet wins victory out of near-defeat by defiant effort. The Self asserts its willingness 'to live it all again/And yet again.' However horrific life may be – and the imagery is powerfully disagreeable – it has value simply as life. In the final stanza the Self is prepared to acknowledge whatever has happened, to look at it fully, and to 'forgive myself the lot!' The last five lines flow freely, leaving behind the imagery of impurity and blindness to reveal the 'sweetness' which results from the act of casting out 'remorse'. Suddenly the pronoun becomes plural: 'We must laught ... We are blest'. The Self is liberated from its isolation and finds itself 'blest by everything' and with the power of blessing other things too. It has even taken over the vocabulary of the – almost forgotten – Soul; the word 'blest' is surely one we would have expected to attribute to spirituality rather than whatever it is that the Self represents. To define that is the final challenge of the poem.

The proper use of cirticism is to help us to see more exactly our own responses to literature. Let us now look at Harold Bloom's comments on the conclusion of the poem in this spirit. Bloom begins by drawing attention to Yeats's belief in the creative power of the imagination, which he sees as solipsistic – based on the belief that 'Self is the only object of real knowledge or the only thing really existent', to give the *OED* definition. He goes on:

> Nothing in the Self's wonderful declaration at the close of 'A Dialogue of Self and Soul' goes beyond re-affirmation of this ecstatic and reductive solipsism, since the source to which every event in action or thought is followed will turn out to be the Self: 'Measure the lot; forgive myself the lot!' We are moved by the reciprocal blessings that follow, and yet we might be a touch uneasy also, for the Self happily is blessing the Self.[13]

He concludes with a reminder of 'how lonely the Yeatsian ecstasy must be':

> The blessing given and taken at the close is hardly a sanctification of the commonplace, as it might have been for Wordsworth, but rather a more intense and less humanly admirable late version of the Sublime mode.[14]

What do you think? It does not seem to me that the state of being evoked at the end of the poem is a lonely one; the Self is now surely involved in a mutually creative relationship with what is around it.

How did it achieve this state? By casting out remorse. Unlike the religious attitude, represented by the Soul, which would no doubt value repentance, the Self can reach 'blessedness' only by getting rid of its sense of guilt. This is what burdens human consciousness, and self-forgiveness rather than forgiveness by some external power is what man needs in order to achieve a positive relationship with the world. This is a kind of humanism which we may see as owing a good deal to Yeats's much earlier enthusiasm for the German philosopher Friedrich Nietzsche. For Nietzsche, as for the Self of this poem, Western civilisation had crippled its citizen-victims by imposing on them a crushing burden of guilty self-condemnation. In reading the 'Dialogue' we share the experience of the Self's self-delivery from that burden, and a rejection of the Soul's spiritual path.

The next poem 'Blood and the Moon', makes powerful use of some of the antitheses of its predecessor, but also brings in a number of new references. Yeats's Note (p. 535–6), which we have already looked at, refers to Shelley's use of towers as symbols: the quotation in Section II is from his *Prometheus Unbound* (1820), IV, 103. The comment that the poem derives in part from Thoor Ballylee's having 'a waste room at the top' and that 'Butterflies come in through the window and die against the window-panes' reminds us of how the poet's imagination was always transforming the ordinary into the significant. Other references are to the lighthouse at Pharos near Alexandria, one of the Seven Wonders of the World, and to the astrological studies of the Babylonians. However, a stronger emphasis in this section (and in later poems, as we shall see) falls on four Irish writers of the eighteenth century: Swift, Goldsmith, Berkeley and Burke.[13]

As a young poet with strong Romantic allegiances, Yeats had despised the eighteenth century, but his attitude changed with the years. When a Senator, he saw the period as one in which the Irish had had a large and successful share in ordering their own affairs. The four writers came to represent for him an impressive Irish tradition of independence and outspokenness to which he aspired to belong. Jonathan Swift (1667–1745) had written powerfully against the English exploitation of Ireland in works like 'A Modest Proposal'. His Latin epitaph in St Patrick's Cathedral, Dublin, where he had been Dean, employs the phrase *saeva indignatio*, 'savage indignation'. A later poem in the volume (p. 277) translates and expands the epitaph. Oliver Goldsmith (1728–74) had written sentimentally but effectively about the depopulation of the country-side in 'The Deserted Village'. George Berkeley (1685–1753), Bishop of Cloyne, was an Idealist philosopher who criticised the empirical trandition of Locke and Hume which Yeats always associated with English materialism. And Edmund Burke (1729–97), referred to earlier in 'The Tower', Part III, had argued for an organic hierarchical society as opposed to modern democratic notions of the state.

Now read the poem, and consider how well these references are integrated into an overall argument. What do you take the main point of the poem to be? (Obviously this has a great deal to do with the antithesis of blood and moon provided by the title).

DISCUSSION

The opening section with its assertive six-syllable lines sets out the meaning being deliberately ascribed to the tower – as pervasive a symbol here as in the volume named after it. It is indeed a 'powerful emblem'. The 'waste room' at the top of the actual tower comes to stand for the failure of the modern world: where there should be a completeness, authority, even light, there is only negation. This failure is contrasted through the imagery of the second section, where the long lines suggest excited affirmative energy.

The poet then declares this tower as his symbol – he is in the tradition he has been defining by example; and the winding stair within the tower he therefore claims too as 'ancestral'. The ancestors whom he then names, however, modify and enlarge the tradition. As is usual in the poetry, as we have seen, the historical references are brought fully to life. The reader can see clearly why the poet wishes to place himself in this tradition. Jonathan Swift is admired for the intensity with which he responded to the human situation as he experienced it; the 'sibylline frenzy blind' is like the trance from which the prophetic Sibyls spoke their cryptic wisdom. (Note the curious way in which as we read Yeats a number of words like 'blind', 'wild', 'lonely', achieve a peculiar positive quality.) Oliver Goldsmith by contrast is admired for his elegance and control – his writings often border on the sentimental, as the honey-pot image suggests. Burke had attacked the 'mechanical' revolutionary view that society can be totally reshaped without causing damage, arguing for gradual evolutionary change by an analogy between the state and natural process ('proved the State a tree'); equality – one of the ideals of the French Revolution – is discredited, seen as only mathematical and dead. Berkeley had argued against Locke that the existence of material objects was only their perception; for him spirit was the only real cause or power. Yeats uses an amusing metaphor – 'this . . . pig of a world' – to dramatise Berkeley's thinking. The final stanza is a summary of all four admired writers. The poet feels allied with these writers – '*our* blood and state' – in their magnanimous concern for the Irish people and their sufferings, and in their Idealism (though it is by no means certain that the others actually shared Berkeley's philosophical outlook). Only God and spirit really exist.

But Yeats knows as well as any of us how contrary to common sense and experience such a belief is, unless we press very hard on the difficult word 'really'. And so the next section, in rhyming eight-syllable lines, contrasts the 'purity of the unclouded moon' with the 'blood-saturated ground' of human experience as represented vividly here in the tower. But if the moon's purity remains 'unclouded', the 'Odour of blood' remains, affecting human beings as it had affected Swift. The 'frenzy' that the poet and his colleagues share with Swift is an expression of the baffled, unfulfillable human desire for the perfection of the superhuman.

The fourth section keeps us within the tower. The beauty of the dead butterflies sustains the note of distress. Then comes the angry question about modern nations. It is not easy to say what answer is given in the last lines. A strong contrast – not unlike that in 'A Dialogue of Self and Soul' – is now developed between 'wisdom' – 'a property of the dead' – and 'power' – 'a property of the living', necessarily stained with blood. The beautiful final image of the moon in 'its' (the poet does not feminise it) glory leaves the world of humanity below in confusion. It would seem that the lack of wisdom in the modern world, even the bloodiness of that world, is nothing unusual or even deserving comment: it is simply the condition in which mankind has to live. The poem ends on this sombre note, the tower having failed to provide a link between the incompatible elements of the poem's title. But the tone remains paradoxically affirmative.

What do you think are the political implications of this poem? Does Yeats's attitude seem to you to have changed in any way since *The Tower*?

DISCUSSION

I think that we have a stronger sense of symbol here, in contrast to history (to use Donoghue's terms). The poet is evidently organising his version of the past in terms of the attitude to Ireland which he now holds – one of greater detachment. He is no longer a Senator. He no longer seems anguished over the failure of the new Ireland to live up to his early hopes. Seeing history as essentially catastrophic, he places his allegiances elsewhere – in the imagination, and in vigorous moment-by-moment living. His mood is less tragic, more triumphantly acceptant of disaster. In terms of practical politics, we may have an uneasy feeling that if wisdom is only for the dead, and its antithesis is power, the world is being abandoned to those with the least inhibited determination to exert authority over others – which in the 1930s led to Fascism. Perhaps Yeats would have replied that it always is.

'Blood and the Moon' is succeeded by six brief, epigrammatic poems, a form less well represented in *The Tower*. The succinctness of these poems makes them all more or less cryptic; the reader is challenged to do a good deal of filling out. Antitheses, as we would by now expect, abound. 'Oil and Blood' is a clear example. The two sections – linked by the rhyme-scheme abcabc – vividly present the contrasting images of the bodies of 'holy men and women' exuding 'Miraculous oil . . .' and those of the vampires, 'full of blood' – so full that the blood soaks the shrouds and even gathers to the lips: the vampires have a disturbing presence, given by that unpleasant final image – perhaps, for all the 'heavy loads of trampled clay' it is the vampires rather than the holy man who will rise again? That disturbing question is brought into the reader's mind, and gives the poem a depth which takes it beyond the merely horrific.

'Veronica's Napkin' too is based on an antithesis, though here the first side occupies six lines, and the contrast only the final rhyming couplet. The opening six lines offer a number of astronomical references.

'The Heavenly Circuit' is the title of Section II, ii of the *Enneads* of the Neoplatonic philosopher Plotinus, to whom several previous references have been made: God is seen as the centre of the Universe, around whom everything circles. Berenice II was an Egyptian queen who offered her hair to the gods for the safe return of her husband, Ptolemy III; it became the constellation *Coma Berenices*. The 'Tent-pole of Eden' is the star above The Garden, on which the heavens – its 'drapery' – depend. A 'needle's eye' is an image of the 'circuit' which is both tiny and huge in its perfection, and can include the Father who created it. These ancient geometrical ideas of the universe are then contrasted with the 'different pole' of Christianity, the cross of Calvary, which produced Veronica's napkin, the handkerchief which, according to the legend, retained the image of Christ's face after he had wiped himself with it on his way to Calvary. Here it is Christianity which is associated with blood. We can see in these poems that Yeats had been taking an interest in the legends of Christianity, but he treats them as having neither more nor less validity than those of any other religious tradition.

In 'Symbols' we encounter a number of familiar references — the tower, the sword, the silk. But the poem is very cryptic. Who are the 'blind hermit' and the 'wandering fool'? In Yeats's strange landscape whatever the watchtower had once been built to protect now seems abandoned. The sword is no longer employed in action, and the final word 'laid' suggests the ending of the tradition which the beauty of the silk had once embodied. A similar though more directly personal feeling may be discerned in 'Spilt Milk', where the clear image of milk disappearing into the stone on which it is spilt gives a sense of the fading of the efforts of the poet and his colleagues — 'We that have done and thought' — into futility.

'The Nineteenth Century and After' was the title of a literary magazine. The poet seizes on its rather downbeat suggestion of decline to assert that the 'great song' of Romanticism has certainly passed; but this poem, unlike its predecessors, finds a paradoxical 'keen delight' in what remains after the nineteenth century, even if that is only the 'rattle of pebbles' under 'the receding wave' of history as the gyre moves to its end. Here Yeats effectively employs a reference to Matthew Arnold's well-known late-Romantic poem, 'Dover Beach', which presents human love as the only value surviving in a world from which 'The Sea of Faith' is receding.

'Statistics' is an attempt at a witty epigram, presumably based on statistics about the relative number of male and female births, and attributing the larger number of the latter to the influence of 'these Platonists', people without sensuality who substitute diagrams for 'God's fire'. If we wanted to offer a sympathetic gloss on the poem, we might point to D. H. Lawrence's *Lady Chatterley's Lover* (1928), a novel admired by Yeats, with its attack on modern 'Platonist' attitudes to the body; he wrote enthusiastically about the novel in two letters to Olivia Shakespeare of May 1933. [16]

In 'Three Movements' we have another pessimistic reading of cultural history: the fish are no doubt the creatures of the literary imagination, vividly alive in their own world in Shakespeare, being trapped by the Romantics who wanted to make didactic uses of them; and finally killed by modern writers — those of the Naturalist tradition? — who feel at home only on the 'land' of the conscious mind, which kills imaginative life.

Something of the same feeling is expressed in 'The Seven Sages', but this time in a dramatic poem of great vivacity and wit. It begins with the first four old men making claims for their association with the great Irish writers of the eighteenth century. The first three make fairly matter-of-fact statements, but the fourth neatly outdoes them with his romantic half-line, 'But mine saw Stella once'. Swift loved Esther Johnson, and his *Journal to Stella* was published posthumously. The fifth Sage asks about the origins of their thoughts, and is answered by the sixth with the view that all the four writers 'hated Whiggery'. The fifth raises the objection that 'Burke was a Whig' (which he was in fact), but this is swept aside by the sixth Sage in true debaterly fashion: all four writers hated Whiggery 'Whether they knew it or not'. He then offers a striking defintion of Whiggery, which is 'levelling' – concerned with equality, 'rancorous' – full of anger against which it sees as privilege, and 'rational' – relying on reason, rather than the imaginative vision of saints, and even drunkards. This is a very 'Irish' rhetoric repudiating the English empirical tradition of rationality and common sense: note that 'rational' is about the most abusive term in the sixth Sage's vocabulary! The seventh agrees, and sees Whiggery as everywhere triumphant in the modern world. Nevertheless, 'we old men' oppose it. The use of the word 'massed' is a splendid piece of rhetoric; seven old men 'massed' against the rest of the world? The absurdity of it is part of the effect. The first four then speak again, each of the writers with whom his ancestor was associated, giving some account of their work or ideas. The work of Goldsmith referred to is 'The Deserted Village', his poem about the depopulation of the Irish countryside. But he had not seen 'the trefoil [the three-leaved clover] stained with blood', the bloodier events of the nineteenth century, or the 'avenging leaf' of Irish Nationalism. The world of Whiggery is now under attack; the ideas of Berkeley, the Bishop of Cloyne, are becoming 'a thunder-clap' warning of imminent change. But the poem ends with the authoritative sixth and seventh Sages. (The fifth, who had asked an awkward question, remains silent.) The seventh explains the 'schooling' of the four great writers. Theirs was evidently the school of experience; they saw the realities of Irish life, turning their mimicry of it into art; and they understood that wisdom does not come from abstract thought but from 'beggary' – the condition of complete exposure to reality. The writer is closer to the child and the beggar than he is to the superior intellectual. 'The Seven Sages' puts Yeats's commitment to his chosen Irish tradition with force and wit.

Do you see this poem as taking up the same position as 'Blood and the Moon'? How is the wisdom won from beggary related to the wisdom that was 'the property of the dead' in the earlier poem?

DISCUSSION

The tradition is clearly invoked with the same enthusiasm, but this poem seems to me to take a more 'political' line. After all, it embodies the view that change is imminent, which to Yeats, who saw modern Western democracy, including the Irish Free State, as decadent and trivialising, was a cause for celebration. To us, looking back to 1933 as the year when Hitler came to power in Germany, it looks disturbingly different. We might also ask how far we are won over to accept the attitude dramatised in the poem. It seems unlikely that those of us, like myself, who attach a higher value to rationality and are more sceptical about the insight of saints and drunkards when so juxtaposed will be convinced; but we will certainly have been led to experience the excitement of this 'Irish' attitude to life.

The next poem, 'The Crazed Moon', would seem at first reading to be taking us into a world of symbols. But in view of our recent consideration of the significance to Yeats of the political events of the 1930s, is it possible to see it in terms of history? I think it is.

The poem, in neat six-line stanzas of flexible syllable numbers, begins dramatically with the moon 'staggering in the sky'; its 'child-bearing' suggests the approaching end of its cycle; the atmosphere is 'Crazed', everything seems to be going out of control. In the atmosphere 'We grope' – the human race is vainly struggling to find something reliable amid their confusion. 'Children born of her pain.' We know that the moon has borne many children; why cannot humanity find them? The second stanza replies that they are 'dazed or dead'. The next two exclamatory sentences evoke the moon's visitation of the earth, and its effects on humanity: it led 'every foot' to participate in 'the dance' – we see something like the savage ritual dance of the followers of Dionysus in 'Two Songs from a Play'. The third stanza offers another perspective: now the human beings are worshipping a vanished goddess; they are seen only in terms of their hands and fingers, stretched out in the moonlight to catch what can never be caught, as the strange opening phrase suggests. Now the tone of the poem becomes even more disturbingly negative. The worshippers – humanity, ourselves – are victims of 'that malicious dream'. The moon is evidently hostile to her worshippers, deliberately misleading them; the participle 'Blanched' neatly encapsulates the visual effect of the moonlight and its moral effect in sapping their selfhood. And so the fingers 'spread wide' are now seen, in the horrific last line, to be trying to 'rend what comes in reach'. No fulfilment being possible for this moon-crazed race, they can only reach out for some form of revenge.

I think you will agree that the poem is vivid and powerful in its almost surreal effects. Can we interpret it in the context? I think we are being encouraged to read it as a comment on the general plight of humanity as Yeats sees it as one cycle of history draws to its close. If we think of the history of Europe at this time, we cannot feel that the nightmare vision was merely the expression of a personal fantasy nor that the poet unequivocally welcomed the change he saw coming.

At all events, we find ourselves back in more recognisably historic territory in the next two poems. 'Coole Park, 1929' and 'Coole Park and Ballylee, 1931' are both written in the dignified eight-line ten-syllable stanza of 'Sailing to Byzantium' and 'Among School Children', and celebrate in elegy the vanished culture represented for Yeats by the home of Lady Gregory,[18] which had been sold to the Forestry Commission in 1927. The earlier poem is another meditation − we have seen Yeats's fondness for this term. The image of the 'swallow's flight' immediately suggests transience, but it is set against the sense of achievement − 'Great works constructed there . . .'; the very walls had the power of begetting. Examples are then given of people associated with Coole: Douglas Hyde, the Gaelic scholar and translator; Yeats himself in his 'manly pose'; the playwright J. M. Synge; and Lady Gregory's two nephews, John Shawe-Taylor, the land reformer, and Hugh Lane, the art collector − 'excellent company' indeed. (Though of course we should not have to rely on the associations of the names to make the poet's point; do you think he conveys why they deserve his high estimation?)

The third stanza opens with a beautiful image linking back to the first, in which the artists, even if working 'in nature's spite', are endowed with the natural elegance of movement of the swallows. But the special quality of Coole Park was that it disciplined its 'swallows' through Lady Gregory's firmness, helping to create 'certainty'. The movement of the birds becomes an emblem of 'intellectual sweetnees'. There is energy and freedom in this movement, somehow enhanced by the culmination of the line in this stanza with 'withershins'. The OED gives two meanings for this word: '1 In a direction opposite to the usual; the wrong way. . . . 2 In a direction contrary to the apparent course of the sun (considered unlucky or causing disaster)'. Which of these seems to you more appropriate? In view of Yeats's interest in astrology, we may be inclined to take the second meaning; but it seems to me that the positive tone of the sentence, its exuberance, leads us to the first definition, omitting the idea of 'the wrong way'. It is a celebration of the power of the intellect to create its own harmonies.

This leads into the final stanza, which directly addresses an appropriate audience of people like those who had once enjoyed the patronage of the house. How does Yeats manage his climactic effect? The sweeping sentence – all eight lines of the stanza – is given impetus by the parallels of the second, third and fourth lines, followed by the imperative verb 'dedicate', which is then skilfully separated from its object – 'A moment's memory . . .' – while the exact scene is evoked. Thus when we reach the last line there is a great sense of completeness. Previously the poetry had evoked the idea of the destruction of the house – like many in Ireland at that time – in vivid images of nettles, saplings and broken stone. Now only memory can give life to what has been destroyed. And so finally the reader, with the traveller, scholar and poet, is told the correct attitude to take up – 'eyes bent upon the ground. . .' – in what is a kind of ritual in which external features of sun and shade must be ignored; he can then pay the appropriate tribute to 'that laurelled head'. Lady Gregory is tactfully not named: that might have a reductive effect. We see her as 'laurelled', rewarded with the recognition of the poet in Greek culture. Why only 'a moment's memory'? I think this is a wonderful piece of poetic tact too: too much is not expected of humanity. There is also the suggestion that, although it is right to commemorate the past, elegy must not turn into nostalgia; the recognition of what has been lost must be converted into a creative energy which will look to the future.

Now read the second Coole poem and formulate your own reactions to it. Do you find it more, or less, impressive? Does it develop beyond the point previously reached?

As we have discussed the earlier poem in detail, I leave you to do this on your own. But I will make one or two observations on particular points which you may feel relevant

DISCUSSION

The first stanza ends with the hyperbolic question, 'What's water but the generated soul?' I wonder whether you agree with me that this is too extravagant to be convincing; water has already been given a realistic presence in the poetry which cannot be swept away by a high-handed claim for the supremacy of symbolism. (The reference to Raftery, the blind – 'dark' – poet of Section II of 'The Tower' who had written in a poem about a pool in the river as the 'cellar' of Ballylee, enforces the historical feeling contradicted here.)

How do you react to the exclamation in the second stanza,

'Another emblem here!' This is another assertion of the power of the mind to use the visible world for its own purposes, which again may strike the reader as reductive. The swan – a favourite image, as we know from 'Nineteen Hundred and Nineteen', Section III, and 'Leda and the Swan'[19] – in its beauty and freedom is evidently symbolic of the soul, which cannot be 'murdered by a blot of ink', whatever the child may believe.

Why do you think Lady Gregory is referred to only through the 'Sound of a stick upon the floor' in the third stanza? On reflection I think you will agree that this is very successful in bringing the reader directly into the situation of the poem. (Lady Gregory was to die in 1932. It is curious that Yeats had effectively written her elegy before the event.)

The last two stanzas develop a view of history and contrast the 'great glory' of the past with the 'shifting' flux of the modern world. How does Yeats see himself in this context, and how convincing do you find his view?

He sees himself with Lady Gregory and the others associated with Coole Park as 'the last romantics'. They had tried to sustain a tradition now destroyed: the 'high horse' of poetry, Pegasus, is now 'riderless', although Homer had been able to mount it by writing his poem about the chaos of the Trojan War. You may feel an effect of strain here, as if the poet is having to try very hard to find a way of conveying his view, and not altogether succeeding.

Do you think that the 'emblematic' meanings ascribed to water and the swan have been assimilated successfully into the argument? I find it difficult to see how. The two planes of the poem remain for me unintegrated. Nevertheless we are left with a powerful sense of the poet's distress as he witnesses the ending of the tradition to which he feels allegiance as both man and poet. Can anything be saved from their destruction?

'For Anne Gregory' certainly saves something in terms of its delightful wit. It takes the form of a dialogue between the poet and Lady Gregory's granddaughter, treating a difficult semi-philosophical question in a human and colloquial way. The poet begins by telling the girl that she can never be loved for herself alone, because her 'yellow hair' will always affect the responses of young men to her. (How banal this sounds in prose! Yet in the lilting rhythm of this poem, I think you will agree that it reads delightfully.) The young woman replies that she could change the colour of her hair. But the poet settles this argument to his own satisfaction, though in a very cavalier fashion, by invoking 'an old religious man' who has found a text proving that no human could do what is God's prerogative, love her for herself alone.

This is a slight poem, to be enjoyed rather than exhaustively analysed. Yet it refers to a really difficult question about human identity. When we love someone, what exactly is the 'self' that we are loving? Is it a 'self alone', with no attributes? Is the 'yellow hair' — synecdoche (the using of a part for the whole) for the whole physical appearance — totally irrelevant? Could a person be the same if his or her appearance were different? Is there an unchanging soul attached to a changing self? The questions are extraordinarily difficult; they are also, as we have seen, of great concern to Yeats. That they lie behind this poem gives it a depth of interest which coheres satisfyingly with its lively and entertaining surface.

Next comes 'Swift's Epitaph', a powerful translation of the Latin epitaph which Swift wrote for himself, and which is inscribed on his tomb in St Patrick's Cathedral, Dublin. The compactness of the form gives the necessary weight. The first line is Yeats's own introduction; thereafter he follows the original, only adding the adjective 'world-besotted'. Note the skill with which the rhythm and punctuation of that last-but-one line lead emphatically into the final one: '*he*/Served human liberty.' By implication the 'world-besotted traveller' does not. It is those who can see further than the material world who truly serve it. Yeats could justifiably see himself in the tradition of Swift in offering his society unpopular truths. 'Savage indignation' is often regarded as a self-indulgence on the part of a writer or social critic; Yeats claims that it does more to further 'human liberty' than conventional politics. He makes the point with admirable economy.

We then leave Ireland and the eighteenth century for a group of poems concerned with more general themes. This begins with 'At Algeciras – a Meditation Upon Death'. The opening stanza seems purely, and attractively, descriptive, despite the poem's title. The 'pale cattle-birds' cross the Straits of Gibralter from Morocco to Spain, and alight there to stay until morning. But the poety has a rich and mysterious effect: the word 'light', apparently an abbreviation, contrasts strangely with the 'rich midnight of the garden trees' which seem to be illuminated, while the 'mingled seas' again sounds romantic and suggestive. In view of the poem's title, we may feel the pale birds as some kind of spiritual messengers. The second stanza offers a reminiscence of childhood, the boy bringing shells to show another friend: but the emphasis on the reality of the shells also serves to draw attention to 'Newton's metaphor' – his famous description of himself as 'a boy playing on the sea-shore, and diverting myself in now and then finding another pebble or prettier shells than ordinary, while the great ocean of truth lay all undiscovered before me.'[20]

The final stanza again begins with natural description, but we may feel the 'evening chill' is that of approaching death. The poet's response is to order his imagination to 'run/Much on the Great Questioner', on the likely questions and the answers he can fittingly give. The tone is calm, acceptant. Death is being envisaged with a tranquillity which draws from the atmosphere of the previous stanzas. The poet is certain that there are some answers he can give 'with a fitting confidence'. This calm assurance of mood makes an attractive contrast with the 'frenzy' with which the idea of death is elsewhere entertained.

'The Choice', by contrast, is a forceful, assertive poem. Man must chose between perfection of life and of work: perfection of life may lead to 'a heavenly mansion' such as that sought by the soul in A Dialogue . . .', but the artist, seeking perfection of work, must take the consequences: the marks of toil, 'an empty purse', days spent in vain activities and nights in remorse for them. This is epigrammatically forceful, showing Yeats's characteristic pleasure in antitheses. But after the gentle meditations of 'At Algeciras' it seems dogmatic, over-simplified: we want to argue back at the poet, whose life was not all vanity and remorse, and who has not, at this period at least, suffered from 'an empty purse'.

'Mohini Chatterjee' is more interesting and suggestive. It is based again on reminiscence: Yeats had met the Indian sage in Dublin in 1885 or 1886, and been very impressed by him. Now he recalls – or perhaps invents – the sage's words in response to the question about prayer, seeing that they were spoken to 'set at rest/A boy's turbulent days'. The words had suggested that man lives many lives. Now the poet feels able to offer his own 'commentary' on them. How cogent do you find that commentary to be? It consists of one sweeping sentence – we have seen how masterly Yeats can be in organising the rhythm of a final sentence into powerful assertion, and the same effect is achieved here. The power of time is denied here: 'Birth-hour and death-hour meet'. The last line re-iterates the point, attributing it to 'great sages' like Chatterjee: 'Men dance on deathless feet'. This is another striking phrase. But how should we interpret it? Does the poem succeed for you in conveying its mysterious wisdom? The answer may depend on your understanding of the position of sages like Chatterjee. I remain puzzled, and think that the poem lacks clarity. But we can see the poet excelling with similar material in the following ambitious and much annotated poem, 'Byzantium'.

It is impossible for readers familiar with 'Sailing to Byzantium' not to see the two poems as related, with the latter adding depth and detail to the account of the symbolic city given in the earlier poem. In fact we know that Yeats wrote 'Byzantium' partly in response to some criticisms by his friend the poet and critic Thomas Sturge Moore on its predecessor.[21]

When Yeats sent Moore a copy of 'Byzantium' to help him in designing the cover for the new volume, he remarked that Moore's criticism had shown him that 'the idea needed exposition'.[22] What kind of exposition does it receive in the new poem? Read the poem carefully before giving your answer.

DISCUSSION

A very powerful exposition, I think you'll agree; and also a difficult and demanding one. 'Byzantium' is a very compressed poem. It consists of five eight-line stanzas – note that Yeats here varies his favourite form once again: now the rhyme-scheme is aabbcddc, with the sixth and seventh lines reduced in length. The effect is authoritative. The first stanza takes us into a world which is simultaneously historical and symbolic: we can envisage the night scene in the ancient city, but the atmosphere generated by the diction, imagery and rhythm is mysterious. There is a sense of the passing of time – day has receded, the soldiers are in bed, the 'night-walkers' song' has followed the curfew gong into silence; all we can perceive is the 'starlit' or 'moonlit' dome – the uncertainty of the 'or' removes the experience from a single occasion into a general condition. The dome is characteristic of Byzantine architecture; most of us have seen, or seen pictures of, the great dome of the Church of Santa Sofia. A dome – unlike the Gothic spire of aspiration – symbolises divinity in its geometrical completeness, and in the cold perfection of the night sky, whether lit by stars or moon, 'disdains/All that man is'. The rhythm places enormous stress on 'disdains', conveying with complete assurance the chilly values of the holy city, contrasted with those of humanity, characterised in terms of 'fury' and 'mire' – powerfully negative words – and by 'mere complexities'. The use of the adjective 'mere' is striking: we often think of complexity as something positive, a sign of human superiority; here it is dismissed as trivial. How much better for man, the argument runs, if he could be purged – see the opening line – of his complexities and achieve a simplicity like that of the disdainful dome.

The second stanza draws us into the very process of purification. In the mysterious night appears an ambiguous presence, 'floating' as manifestations of the supernatural are often said to do. It is 'an image', associated with man and his shadow, but now having its own vitality. It is evidently involved in unwinding 'the winding path' of life; 'bound in mummy-cloth' – we are reminded of 'All Souls' Night' – it is 'Hades' bobbin'. Hades is the classical Underworld to which spirits pass after death; the bobbin is the weaver's tool. The suggestion is of a being engaged after death in the process of experiencing again, in reverse, all the events of its life. Its mouth is without moisture and breath, the signs of life, and so it can summon other 'Breathless' spirits. The poet responds with excitement: 'I hail the superhuman'. The interchangeable phrases of the next line (eerily reminiscent of Part III of Coleridge's *The Ancient Mariner* in which the mariner encounters 'the nightmare Life-in-Death') help to explain the excitement: for here the most basic of all antitheses, the one so frequently worrying the ageing Yeats, seems to have been resolved.

We move further into the strange topography of the night-bound city in the next stanza, with its focus on a perfect work of Byzantine art, the miraculous golden bird on its golden bough. (You may have recognised the phrase *The Golden Bough* as the title of Sir James Frazer's great work of anthropology, which appeared between 1890 and 1915: Yeats knew the work and was interested in its ideas. This use of the phrase here is perfectly appropriate to the scene described, but I think he would also have enjoyed the idea of the Frazer reference as one particularly likely to appeal to scholars.) There are two possibilities for the cock: if in star light (associated by Yeats with Phase 1 of *A Vision*, the dark of the moon), it may crow 'like the cocks of Hades', a positive response suggesting the possibility of rebirth; or if in moonlight (Phase 16, the full of the moon) it will, like the dome of stanza 1, express its scorn for the complexities of the natural world.

The strangest scene of all is reserved for midnight, the time traditionally associated with the spirit world. What we have is simultaneously a vivid description of the marble mosaics constituting the floor of the central place of the sacred city, and an enactment of an extraordinary ritual. The vowel sounds of words like 'flit', 'flames', 'steel', 'lit', and the marked alliteration all highlight the mystery. These flames are spiritual, 'begotten of flame' not of faggots. The length of the sentence keeps us within the experience of the 'blood-begotten spirits' – for however much the spirits may wish to achieve purity, they cannot deny their human origins in blood – as they 'die' into the dance. The last three lines enact the dance, which is also a trance, and an agony: an agony the spirits are prepared to endure to enter the world of Byzantine perfection.

The last stanza opens with two exclamations, showing the poet's excitement at what he is seeing. The dolphins which traditionally brought the dead to the Islands of the Blest, and are often portrayed in Byzantine mosaics, are physical beings. But the poem is celebrating the defeat of the physical by the 'golden smithies of the Emperor'. The smithies which produce the golden birds and boughs, and are of course associated with fire, 'break the flood'. Art, the imagination, can triumph over nature, giving it whatever forms it chooses. The final sentence gives great emphasis to the repeated word 'break' at the beginning of the fifth line. Still the tone is exultant: more so than in the more neutrally descriptive use of the word in the second stanza of 'Coole Park and Ballylee, 1931'. But there is surely something questionable about the phrase: can one *break* a flood? No doubt the use of it here is deliberately rhetorical, making extreme claims for the power of the imagination. Nevertheless it seems to me that some kind of duality begins to build up in the reader at this point, and continues into the wonderfully emphatic last line. The syntax is hard to follow. Presumably 'those images' and what come after are all in apposition to 'bitter furies of complexity', all part of what the marbles 'break'. And yet they seem to gather a vitality of their own. 'Images' – a key word in the poem – can 'beget' other images from the sea, which we cannot help seeing as a symbol of life. And 'begetting' is itself a characteristic of living. If the argument of the poem is to assert the power of art over life, it is paradoxical that our last thought is of the uncontrollable power of the sea.

This poem has been discussed by the many major modern critics. Let us look at some of their views about the conclusion of the poem to see whether they can help us to form our own view more exactly. G. S. Fraser writes thus of the final stanza:

> Here . . . we are told that the representation of the flux, on the marble floor, controls the flux. But it is the real flux, with all its terror and fertility, not the represented one, that we are suddenly presented with: it is as if the sea of Marmara was suddenly overflowing the mosaic sea on the marble floor, real dolphins bouncing above the mosaic dolphins. The gong is the great cathedral gong of the first stanza; it is only a real sea, not a marble sea, that its beatings could torment or disturb.[23]

Frank Kermode, though equally aware of the teachings dramatised in the poem as a whole, sees the overall significance differently:

> The focus of attention is no longer [as it was in 'Sailing to Byzantium'] on the poignancy of the contrast between nature and art in these special senses; nature now becomes 'mere complexities,/The fury and the mire' and the strategy of the poem is, clearly, to establish the immense paradoxical vitality of the dead, more alive than the living; still, but richer in movement than the endless agitation of becoming.[24]

F. A. C. Wilson in *Yeats and Tradition* (1958) takes a different approach again. His main argument is that Yeats should be seen in relation to what he terms 'The Subjective Tradition' of Platonism, Neoplatonism, the Jewish Kabbala and other mystical works. 'Byzantium' is therefore discussed in terms of Platonic symbolism, with the result that the city is held to be a symbol of the life after death. But at the end of the poem the narrator, having had his glimpse of the purity of heaven, is returned to the world:

> It is therefore apt that his eyes should close upon the vision of the sea of life, for this is the condition to which, with consciousness, he will be restored. As for the meaning of the last line, with its wealth of symbolic detail . . . The sea is 'torn' by dolphins and reverberates with the echoes of St. Sophia's gong; the surface of man's life is split asunder by the passion of love and the desire for perfection, and is endlessly tormented by the idea of death.[25]

Finally, you might like to bear in mind the ingenious suggestion of Kenneth Burke that we detect behind that last line of the poem 'a strange heresy disguised, by the enigma of the pun. Might we hear instead: "That devil-torn, that God-tormented sea?"'[26]

   Perhaps that is going too far, but I think you will agree that the other three critics do help to focus our attention usefully. I find myself closest to Fraser, because I think he gives the best account of the unexpectedness of the ending. I wonder whether you would regard it as a flaw in the poem that argument should turn back in this way on itself?

'The Mother of God' is a short dramatic monologue in which Mary considers the implications of having been chosen to take on the astonishing role of the poem's title. The poem is very successful in imaginatively exploring Mary's consciousness, in making us look carefully at a state of being which is easily simplified into emptiness by the common use of the little phrase, especially in Roman Catholicism. Here Yeats invests a theological phrase with human feeling. Can you see any relation between the poem and those immediately before and after it? (We will return to this question).

   The title 'Vacillation' would seem to give the poet the opportunity of investigating further aspects of the dialectic which we have found so frequently in the volume. It makes use in the second section of a mythological tree from the collection of Welsh romances called *The Mabinogion*, which Yeats admired, consisting of flame and leaf. There is also a reference to 'Attis' image'. Attis is a Greek vegetation god who became a pine tree after death. During the festival of Attis, according to Frazer in *The Golden Bough* (1890), I, 297–9, the effigy of a young man was attached to a pine

tree to suggest his return to life in the form of a tree. The sixth
section quotes briefly from a Chinese statesman and writer, the
'great lord of Chou'. The final section is addressed to Friedrich von
Hügel, a Catholic philosopher whose work Yeats admired, but with
whom he must finally disagree. He can quote scripture, but not to
embrace Christianity. In *Judges* 14, Samson kills a lion and later
finds a honeycomb in its carcass. From this he makes up the
riddle:'Out of the eater came what is eaten, and out of the strong
came what is sweet'. Presumably for Yeats the two elements remain
disunified. Similarly, the poet and the orthodox philosopher must
part.

Now read the poem. What is the poet vacillating between, and
how is the vacillation resolved?

DISCUSSION

The cryptic opening section in short, emphatic lines sets man
'Between extremities', which only death, physically, or remorse,
spiritually, can destroy. The 'antinomies' which we have seen in so
many of the poems will then disappear. But what will then happen
to joy? Is it the product of the tension?

The second section describes the mythological tree and takes
us into a world of primitive ritual. To participate in such a ritual, it
would seem, is to solve the problem.

The third section begins with a stanza of advice, expressed
with vigour, about worldly success; but then more pathetically
notes the paradoxes of life, and the inadequacy of human
relationships to fully satisfy human longings. That the advice is self-
addressed becomes clear in the second stanza, where the by now
familiar subject of preparation for death is introduced. 'Lethean
foliage' enabled one to forget reality. Now, in the knowledge of
that reality, the poet confidently asserts that only certain kinds of
creative work are worthwhile, defining their qualities in terms of
their appropriate audience – 'men as come/Proud, open-eyed and
laughing to the tomb'. These seem to have real experience of joy in
life, such that they approach death with no fear.

Is the poet one of these men? The fourth section consists of an
autobiographical story. It begins simply, the poet alone in a London
tea-shop; suddenly, inexplicably, he experiences a state of ecstasy.
The poetry conveys this in its simple, vivid diction and imagery –
'My body . . . blazed' – and the half-repetition of the last line.
However, as we look back we see the emphatic word 'seemed' near
the start of the penultimate line, and wonder how much of a reality
the blessed state was.

The next section strikes a contrary note. Here the poet is so
weighted down by 'Responsibility' that he cannot respond to the
beauty of sunlight or moonlight. There is no escape in the second
stanza, which wearily repeats the poet's sense of failure. His
memories are only of events 'appalling' to either conscience or
vanity. The flatness of this leads the reader on the seek some
solution or escape.

The sixth section provides this by quoting words attributed to
the 'great lord of Chou'. The words, 'Let all things pass away,' are
then repeated as a kind of chorus to the two following verses, as if
they provide some consolation for the transience of things. But of
course they do not in any way resolve the problem; they merely will
what is already the case. Perhaps this is all we need to do? The
increasingly bitter tone of the poem, the reference in the third
stanza to 'man's blood-sodden heart' (reminiscent of Swift in earlier
poems), make the solution seem desperate rather than satisfying.

The seventh section is more balanced and detached, as Soul
and Heart continue the argument of the earlier 'Dialogue'. The Soul
is confident as to what reality is, something to be experienced in a
spirit like that of Isaiah, who was purified by an angel who touched
his lips with a coal. But the Heart, speaking for the poet, fears that
such salvation can lead only to dumbness. His final question asserts
that the poet must follow Homer in writing about the sinfulness of
man, and by implication that he must live in a way which shares
this basic human characteristic too. The possibility of a religious art
is rejected.

The eighth and final section is written in a lively and
magnanimous spirit. The long, swinging lines enact a friendly
relationship between the poet and the man he is addressing, von
Hügel. At first the poem emphasises their points of agreement:
Yeats believes in the supernatural, accepts the belief that when the
tomb of St Theresa of Avila was opened, her body was undecayed
and exuded beautiful perfume. He can believe in reincarnation.
Nevertheless, he has to dissociate himself from the Catholic
thinker. Christianity may offer a belief that seems 'most welcome in
the tomb' – because of the promise of resurrection? – but the poet
must play his 'predestined part', following the example of Homer.
The lilt of the last line – with the poet ironically 'blessing' the
religious thinker – concludes the poem on an agreeable human
note.

How do you see this poem in relation to those previously
looked at?

It is clearly another contribution to the continuing debate of
which 'Byzantium' provided – or tried to provide – one answer.

'Vacillation' points in the opposite direction. Rather than committing himself to perfection, the poet chooses the fallen world. Only by living in it can he attempt to mount the 'high horse' whose 'saddle Homer road', Homer representing in these poems the true poetic spirit which immerses itself in life.

Can we now fit in 'The Mother of God'? It presents another perspective by emphasising the possible human cost of having to bear witness too supernatural values. Though again I would emphasise that we should not allow our interest in seeking a pattern for the whole volume to narrow our reading of specific poems. In this case, nothing should distract us from Yeats's unusual sensitivity to Mary's humanity.

Now read through the next five poems, up to 'Stream and Sun at Glendalough'. Do you see any common features?

DISCUSSION

They seem to me to have a considerable autobiographical element, with the poet thinking of old friends, and his career as an Irish poet. The culminating statement of 'Remorse for Intemperate Speech' is a bitter assertion of the constricting influence of the political legacy of Ireland. But the 'I' of the final poem escapes momentarily into gaiety as he looks with 'attention' at the world of stream and sun. He is distracted by 'repentance' which 'keeps my heart impure' — paradoxically, because it is the impurity of the heart which originally prompts it. The question then put to the self shows the poet in an unusually humble mood. The man who has so often lauded 'pride' now asks how he *dare* feel himself superior. The last stanza answers the question only with further questions. The poet can only seek to discover the source of his brief joy, but there is no doubt of the intensity of that joy while it lasted, conveyed in the physical stress in 'pierced my body through'. There had been some cooperation of sun, stream and eyelid, of nature and man. For a moment he had lived 'like these', the stream and sun, 'That seem/ Self-born, born anew'. Of course we can give an historical account of these things. But that would be to miss the point. At one particular moment of the poet's experience he had felt the vitality of nature in its 'intricate motion', shared the creatvity, lost his sense of self-importance. But the moment has passed, the complexity of life has reasserted itself; he is 'a common man' after all. The poem does not attempt the philosophical answers of some of the more ambitious poems, but movingly conveys the sense of a man briefly released through a particular quality of attention to a nature from the winding stairs of human impermanence.

The volume does not finish here, however; we still have two further sequence series of poems, 'Words for Music Perhaps' and 'A Woman Young and Old'. The title of the latter reminds us of the sequence in *The Tower* entitled 'A Man Young and Old'. Yeats's Note tells us that it was 'written before the publication of *The Tower*, but left out for some reason I cannot recall' (p. 536). He gives a fuller account of the genesis of the first sequence; saying how he was suddenly filled with 'an impression of the uncontrollable energy and doing of the great creators' which might destroy the world itself. He began with 'Mad as the Mist and Snow' and then wrote most of the others in the group called 'Words for Music Perhaps' 'in memory of those exultant weeks' (p. 537), though later adding some others in the same mood.

The word 'exultant' offers a starting-point from which we may view the sequence of powerful lyric poems. The first seven employ the persona of Crazy Jane, an aged peasant-woman like Moll Magee of the early ballad (pp. 25–7) or 'old Madge' and Margery of 'A Man Young and Old'. The form, with its free use of repetition and chorus, suggests the folk tradition. There are three principal characters, Jane, her dead lover Jack the Journeyman, and her respectable old acquaintance who is now the Bishop. How do you understand these three characters and the relationship between them?

DISCUSSION

The two men – 'The solid man and the coxcomb' – represent antithetical human qualities of mind and body. Jane, it soon becomes evident, prefers the latter, the physical. The theme is presented in several different ways but always with the same evaluation. The dialectic becomes increasingly a matter of assertion and denial, as in the sixth poem, describing Jane's final encounter with her old opponent, now the Bishop. He gives her spiritual advice, drawing attention with unepiscopal indelicacy to her physical decline. But she is given two stanzas in which to reply, and has the better of the exchange. She believes that 'fair needs foul', that we cannot simplify life. In language of great physicality she discusses the sexual act from the woman's point of view, arguing that our physical natures disprove the Bishop's implied belief in a purity which avoids the necessity for 'rending' as part of the passion of love. Do you feel that the outspoken reference to 'the place of excrement' is too distasteful for us to go with Jane's view? I think it is well balanced in the otherwise dignified diction. The whole argument is that the 'heavenly mansion' of conventional religion is an evasion; Love has 'pitched his mansion' in the least dignified part of the human body. Only when we have accepted that can we begin to live with full honesty. The shocking effect is necessary here.

The last of Jane's poems shows her, old, having a vision of young dancers. Their dance – that of an 'ivory image' and 'her chosen youth' – is a strange and violent one. The youth seems about to strangle the girl with her own hair: the girl draws a knife to kill the youth. The old woman does nothing to interfere in their case; she is so struck by the gleam of 'Eyes and eyelids'; she is convinced that 'They had all that had their hate'. The chorus-line sums it up: 'Love is like the lion's tooth', savage and dangerous. In the last stanza Jane wonders whether either or both had actually died, and then completely dismisses the question. She can recall when she was young and cared nothing at all – a 'thraneen' is dialect for a blade of grass – for anything but the physical ability to participate in 'Such a dance as there was danced'. This dance of physical passion, however dangerous, has an unforgettable intensity not to be found elsewhere – certainly not in the Christian tradition.

Such is the argument of the group of poems. What do you think of it? The vigour of the poems themselves, and the fact that Jane largely presents her own case, lead us to follow her closely. But we may wish to resist the extreme position – the physical, not the spiritual – to which we are being led. Indeed Yeats offers us an escape by attributing these views to a character acknowledged to be crazy. With an evasiveness that is, we have seen, characteristic not only of Yeats but of poetic discourse itself, the poet gives us his characters enacting their roles, dramatising their views, leaving us to decide the appropriate response.

We may feel something crude about the position represented by Crazy Jane. Perhaps that is why Yeats follows up with a group of seven poems, tender in tone, in which the protagonists are a Girl and a Young Man. Read these poems; do you see them as thematically linked?

DISCUSSION

The same underlying question about reality can be discerned: can love enable human beings to cope with the inevitability of death? The Girl is the less confident of the two, expressing her view with particular poignancy in 'Her Anxiety', to which 'His Confidence' surely seems an inadequate reply.

Do the last two poems in the group, 'Her Dream' and 'His Bargain', offer a positive answer? The dream is certainly of an affirmative kind. Berenice's hair, as we saw in connection with 'Veronica's Napkin', is a constellation which symbolises fidelity. The fact that she sees the hair 'burning' suggests that the sacrifice to love has been recognised and rewarded in the spectacle. The bargain is more mysterious. 'Plato's spindle' no doubt refers to 'the spindle of Necessity' in Book X of *The Republic*, on which 'all the revolutions [of the universe] turn'. The feeling is not of classical order, but rather of the chaos of things, of a world in which the fictitious and unattractive figures of 'Dan and Jerry Lout' behave with casual promiscuity. But the conclusion asserts the Young Man's repudiation of all this; he is not to be affected by the whirling of the threads, because he has made his 'bargain with that hair/And all the windings there'. He has committed himself without reservations to the woman's hair – metonymy for her beauty, and inseparable from her selfhood (as 'For Anne Gregory' suggested). All 'the windings there' remind us of the prevailing metaphor of the volume, and of the essential complexity of life, which the Young Man in his full insight accepts, whatever the cost. Thus the group ends on a note of positive commitment.

Then follow several separate lyrics. 'Three Things' uses the refrain effectively to contrast the bone, 'wave-whitened' on the shore, with its vivid memories of life. 'Cruel death', we know, will not surrender what it has gathered in, but the poetic imagination can briefly loosen its grasp. It does so here in the three recalled scenes: with a child, with a man, and as lover. (The difference between the second and third memories is that in the first the woman remembers the pleasure she gave to men, and in the second her own satisfaction with 'my rightful man'. The post-coital stretching and yawning gives a great sense of sensual fulfilment.) The use of the refrain adds poignancy to the bone's requests. In the last line, the sensuality is replaced by its opposite, and with that emphasis on death the poem closes. But the voice of the bone, once heard, cannot be negated.

'Lullaby' is an attractive love lyric. Our expectation that it will be addressed to a child, perhaps sharpened by the expression 'where you fed', is replaced, through the reference to Paris and Helen, and later to other lovers, by the idea of the lover feeding metaphorically on the semi-maternal comfort of the woman. The tone is tender, protective. The simple language makes the romantic Trojan world seem convincing and probable without losing any of its glamour. The second stanza invokes another famous pair of lovers, this time medieval, Tristram and Isolde, whose love was made irresistible by the magic potion which they drank. The last three lines are wonderfully creative of a sense of natural vitality in roe and doe, in oak and beech, in leaping and running; the exchange of the activities of roe and doe sustaining the sense of mutual loving completeness.

Finally we return to Yeats's favourite classical legend, the scene on the bank of the Spartan river Eurotas where Zeus came to Leda. We have of course encountered that scene already in 'Leda and the Swan'. But how different the effect here. Instead of violence, we have gentleness; 'that brute blood of the air' is here 'the holy bird'; and the scene ends not with the 'indifferent beak' of the departing swan god, but the 'protecting care' of the woman. The earlier poem is far better known than this one, yet 'Lullaby' is a masterly articulation of tender human concern. Yeats could express both moods, but our modern consciousness is drawn more to the scene of violence and outrage.

'After Long Silence' and 'Mad as the Mist and Snow' – which Yeats called 'a mechanical little song' (Note p. 537) – are concerned with what art can offer humanity. 'Bodily decrepitude is wisdom' because in it false reliance on the physical is impossible; but neither Cicero nor Homer is exempt from the 'mist and snow', the chaos of human history. But even if 'Those Dancing Days are Gone', the old man need no longer pretend but can sing to both young and old of the power of the imagination: 'I carry the sun in a silver cup/The moon in a silver bag'. The dancing reference is continued in the next two poems. 'I am of Ireland', as Yeats's Note tells us, is 'developed from three or four lines of an Irish fourteenth-century dance song' (p.535). The male observer here refuses to join the dance, and contrasts strongly with the protagonist of 'The Dancer at Cruachan and Cro-Patrick'. (The reference is to Croagh Patrick, Patrick's Leap, a place of pilgrimage for Catholics in County Mayo.) This dancer is ecstatic, his dance enacting the physical existence of all creation, whose vitality is a tribute to 'Him', the force behind all this activity.

The doctrine of this poem, its exuberant vitality, links it to the next group of poems, the three attributed to Tom the Lunatic. Despite his name – or because of it, if we recognise the positive implications of craziness and lunacy throughout this sequence – Tom is concerned with issues that we may term metaphysical or theological. In the first poem he is singing of the change in him which has been brought about by age, the decline of his faculties. He does not doubt that Nature's light is essentially unchanging, though he can no longer perceive it clearly. The second stanza begins with a rather jolly rhythm, affirming that Tom's companions and occupations – wenching and drinking – 'still remain'; but he has another kind of vision in which these characters appear to be dead. In an uncomfortable phrase, his 'eyeballs' have grown weary. However, Tom's poem ends in a powerful assertion. The assertion has two elements: firstly, that every living creature, including man, 'Stands in God's unchanging eye'. In what we may see as a vision of Berkeley's philosophy, the eye of God is what guarantees existence. Secondly, each creature 'stands' – the repetition of the word gives physicality; we are not discussing essences – 'In all the vigour of its blood'. God's eye does not reduce the physicality of the creatures which it contemplates: blood is essential to life. That Tom lives *or dies* in 'that faith' is a neat conclusion: he will not allow his failing senses or the approach of death to undermine his belief in what life necessarily is.

'Tom at Cruachan' takes us back to the scene of poem XXI. Now Tom is sleeping, and formulating in his mind the profound and disturbing truth which appears in the striking imagery of the last three lines. The world is 'the foal' born of the intercourse of Eternity and Time. The physicality of the image gives what might be an abstract idea great vividness.

In 'Old Tom Again' we have his last insight. He is still confident, assertive. The first two lines provide a fine image of beauty and achievement in the 'swelling canvas'. This is then equated with 'the self-begotten', an important idea for Yeats, implying the ability of consciousness to transcend the empirical. The objects in the last two lines refer to the processes of production, destruction and reproduction, but they are given credence only by 'fantastic men'. Tom neatly subverts our usual notions about fantasy and reality, stating categorically that it is 'the self-begotten' which will endure and succeed, while the 'realistic' beliefs of empiricists are more fantastic.

The last poem 'The Delphic Oracle upon Plotinus', appropriately deals with death, but it does so in a manner which is simultaneously learned and relaxed. The Delphic Oracle was believed by the ancient Greeks to have supernatural authority. In a story with which Yeats was clearly familiar, the philosopher Porphyry has Amelius consult the Oracle to learn what has happened to the soul of Plotinus after death. (The story can be found, among other places, in Stephen MacKenna's translation *Plotinus; the Ethical Treatises* (1917), pp. 22–3.) But the words of the Oracle as given in the poem are descriptive rather than explanatory. The neat five-line stanza with its regular rhyme succinctly describes the philosopher struggling through the salt sea. Rhadamanthus, the son of Zeus and Europa, was a judge in the region of Elysium, to which those favoured by the gods would pass after death. He beckons Plotinus, suggesting that he is destined for salvation, but remains blandly unperturbed by Plotinus's struggle in the buffeting sea. The 'salt blood' which impairs his vision suggests unpurged physicality.

The second stanza is elegant in its movement as it discloses the Elysian scene. We see some of the saved: Plato, Minos – Rhadamanthus' brother, Pythagoras (associated with music in 'Among School Children'), and 'all the choir of Love'. How relaxed and pleasurable it sounds! But doesn't the reader have a slight sense of absurdity too? Is this *all* that these great creatures of the Golden Race have to do to pass their time? As we look back at the struggling Plotinus, the elegance of Elysium becomes disturbing, particularly because of the bland indifference of those there to the one struggling to reach it. As so often, the poet disturbs our expectations, establishing a characteristic tension between feelings about perfection and effort. The poem brings the whole sequence to an end on a deftly subversive note.

What did you think of the sequence as a whole? you see all the poems as belonging together? Was it appropriate to end with Plotinus? At this stage it seems quite reasonable to leave these questions to you. But I do enjoy the comic effect of placing the philosopher Plotinus in company such as that of Crazy Jane and Tom the Lunatic.

The final sequence we encounter, 'A Woman Young and Old', had, as mentioned before, been written earlier than the other poems in this volume. We might see it as a counterpart to 'A Man Young and Old' in *The Tower*, and its use of a chorus from Sophocles in the concluding poem reminds us of that volume too. The poems vary a good deal in their scope and depth, with a general movement, appropriate to the ageing of the protagonist, towards greater complexity. In the 1929 New York edition of *The Winding Stair* Yeats provided an explanation of some of the imagery and references of the sequence. The Note is dated Rapallo, March 1928:

> I have symbolised a woman's love as the struggle of the darkness to keep the sun from rising from its earthly bed. In the last stanza of The Choice [now 'Chosen', p. 311] I change the symbol to that of the souls of man and woman ascending through the Zodiac. In some Neoplatonist or Hermetist – whose name I forget – the whorl changes into a sphere at one of the points where the Milky Way crosses the Zodiac.[27]

The Note in the *Collected Poems* simply states: 'The "learned astrologer" in 'Chosen' was Macrobius' – Macrobius's commentary of *Scipio's Dream* is then quoted (p. 536). According to this, the soul is descending, and is drawn out of the divine sphere into an imperfect cone.

All this makes it sound as if the sequence will be heavily intellectual. Is this your impression?

DISCUSSION

Not, I would think, of the majority of the poems, which are often lyrical and direct. However, 'Chosen' is, as we have just seen, a poem with a philosophical background. It is a highly-wrought poem in an unusual nine-line stanza modelled on John Donne's reflective poem, 'A Nocturnal Upon St Lucie's Day'. The woman speaker takes us into an astronomical world, but its basic assertion is contained in the definiteness of the opening sentence: the 'lot of love' is not a matter of chance – it is not a lottery; it is chosen. There is a mysterious correspondence betwwen the two lovers, expressed in imagery associating the male figure with the sun. F. A. C. Wilson in *W. B. Yeats and Tradition* relates the poem to Yeats's overall philosophical position, and describes the poem as offering 'the counter-truth to his [Donne's] catalogue of love's "privations".'[28] The speaker triumphs over 'the horror of daybreak' by deliberately choosing it. She can now recall, and tell other brides of, the 'stillness' of achieved mutuality between the man and herself, where a perfection, imaged in the sphere, is achieved, which takes those experiencing it beyond the confines of time, imaged in the zodiac. Whether the 'learned astrologer' was Macrobius matters far less than the sense of fulfilment in choosing to accept the reality of passion.

'Parting' is a poignant dialogue, a little like that of the lovers in Shakespeare's *Romeo and Juliet* III, v. The lover thinks that he must leave, the woman wants him to remain. To him the bird is the herald of dawn, to her 'love's bird', the nightingale, reproving the approach of day: 'murderous stealth' brilliantly conveys her sense of its ineluctable destructive advance. For her, the moon is still in the ascendant; whatever the man may say, she will keep him by offering her 'dark declivities'. This Latinate word, meaning 'Downward slope' (OED), gives a quietly mysterious ending, dignifying her offer beyond ordinary sexuality.

But the most powerful poem in the sequence seems to me 'Her Vision in the Wood'. Here the woman is old and the scene mysterious; we find ourselves in a mythical world which reminds us of the first of the 'Two Songs from a Play' in *The Tower*. We are back in the familiar ten-syllabled eight-line stanza, with a concluding couplet, used in 'Sailing to Byzantium', and always giving leisurely authority. The old woman remembers standing in a sacred wood at midnight, tortured by sexual desire, inflicting pain on herself for distraction or to see that she still has red blood within. It is an horrific scene. As she stares at the blood on her fingers, she suddenly becomes aware of action, light, a 'deafening music'. A group of men come in, bearing a litter with a man fatally wounded by some animal of the wood. The reader will probably recognise that this is like the famous classical story of Venus and Adonis, in which the goddess of love sees her handsome lover killed by a savage boar. The movement of the poetry, the elaboration of the final couplet, give the scene a feeling of ritual; this is continued in the opening of the third stanza describing the stately women mourners in terms of Italian Renaissance art, particularly that of Andrea Mantegna. The woman cannot remain detached, however; she finds herself drawn into the emotion of the scene, singing her 'malediction' with the others. The word is significant: the feeling is not elegiac but angry. In the powerful last stanza the dying man – horrifically described – turns his eyes upon the woman: and she recognises him. The mourners see nothing of what happens to her. But she falls, shrieking, having recongised in the man 'no fabulous symbol', not something in the dead world of classical allusion after all, but, astonishingly, 'my heart's victim and its torturer'. The effect is suddenly and dramatically to draw us away from myth into the intensely personal. The man is both victim and torturer; in this bleak vision, love is an irresistible attraction which destroys all those who are drawn into it. But the recognition of this truth carries the pleasure of sudden illumination.

The sequence ends with a translation of the Fourth Ode in Sophocles' tragedy *Antigone*, in which the Chorus laments the inexorable power of love, which is leading Antigone to her death. Yeats makes the mood imperative, calling upon the power of love to destroy. Love is a 'great glory', but it shows its power through destruction. The final lines lament the forthcoming death of Antigone. Her descent into 'the loveless dusk', the effect of finality enhanced by the rhyme, brings the poem, sequence and volume to a powerful and sombre consclusion. Death, not love, has the last word.

Do you think it would have made any difference to our reading experience if Yeats had followed chronology and placed ' Woman Young and Old' before 'Words for Music Perhaps'? Do you see the two sequences as linked with the main group of poems in significant ways?

DISCUSSION

I think we can see that the continuity of concern is there: Self and Soul continue to find various voices throughout the volume. By concluding with 'From the "Antigone"' rather than 'The Delphic Oracle' or 'Stream and Sun' Yeats asserts the negative pole of his dialectic. Yet the dialectic force and energy remains, for the destruction recorded by Sophocles was the result of being driven wild 'By that great glory' of Antigone's human commitment. Imaginative energy both expresses and resists the power of the 'loveless dust'.

How are we to characterise *The Winding Stair* compared to its predecessor? We saw at the beginning of this chapter that Yeats himself thought of *The Tower* as bitter, and hoped to write more 'amiably'. Thomas Parkinson puts the point authoritatively: 'he made a fierce effort to cast out remorse ("Repentance keeps my heart impure") and affirm passion, so that *The Winding Stair* can

Yeats broadcasting from a B.B.C. Studio, 1936

very profitably be read as reaction to *The Tower*'.[29] Nevertheless, as we have seen, the affirmation of passion is made against an overwhelming sense of the inevitability of death. It is because the world of the swordsman and the lover is necessarily transient that the affirmations of its value are always made on the edge of desperation. The 'personality' of the volume, to revert to Donoghue's term, may be less bitter than that of *The Tower* but it would be misleading to exaggerate the difference. If the earlier volume was, in Donoghue's words already quoted, 'symbolism glancing ruefully at history', *The Winding Stair*, in both its central image and its specific meditations, once again dramatises the aspirations of the symbolic imagination which cannot avoid the experience of history and may at times be able to celebrate that experience.

5   Conclusions and Suggestions

Yeats was to go on to publish two further volumes, *Parnell's Funeral and Other Poems* (1935) and *New Poems* (1938), which 'concluded' characteristically with the question 'Are you Content?' (pp. 370–1). He had also planned a further volume to include his last poems, together with the plays *Purgatory* and *The Death of Cuchulain*, when he died in 1939; this was published by the Cuala Press in Dublin in 1939 as *Last Poems and Two Plays*. Unfortunately the 1950 Macmillan edition of the *Collected Poems* prints these as a continuation of *New Poems*, and not in the order Yeats had planned, which begins with 'Under Ben Bulben' (pp. 397–401) and concludes with 'Politics' (pp. 392–3). This is particularly regrettable in the case of a poet who, as we have seen, gave so much thought to the planning of each volume.[1]

I would suggest that when you have time you read through these three collections and formulate your own ideas about the 'personality' of each. Perhaps you might find it stimulating in your efforts to do so to bear in mind Yeats's statement in 'The Circus Animals' Desertion' (pp. 391–2) that the poems originate somewhere in 'the foul rag-and-bone shop of the heart'. What kind of poetry could emerge from such a view of the human heart? Those of you who have particularly enjoyed the play of the Yeatsian dialectic will note the striking contrast between the spokesman of 'The Gyres', opening the 1938 volume in a mood of superhuman exaltation, and that of 'Politics', ending the 1939 volume in a confession of irresponsible humanity.

You may want also to go back to earlier volumes, making your own assessment of their 'personalities' and in particular the relationship in them between symbol and history. You may find there is more to be said in favour of an early volume like *The Rose*, or a middle-period volume like *Responsibilities*. You may also want to reconsider Yeats's remark (quoted on p. 58 above) about his continuity of concern: 'What man is this who ... says the same thing in so many different ways? ... The swordsman throughout repudiates the saint, but not without vacillation'. Do you find yourself entering a restricted world as your read? Are you led to agree with Eliot's 1919 criticism that Yeats's mind is 'in some way independent of experience'? Or Leavis's view that only in 'Among School Children' does Yeats achieve full poetic authority? My view is that we often find ourselves entering the world of central human concerns, which is where we expect great literature to lead us.

Here, though, to end on are two contrasting judgments by the poets I began by describing as being, with Yeats, the 'founding fathers of modern English poetry'.

Following Yeats' death in 1939, T. S. Eliot was invited by the Friends of the Irish Academy to deliver the first Annual Yeats Lecture at the Abbey Theatre in Dublin, on 30 June, 1940. He concluded his lecture with these words:

> There are some poets whose poetry can be considered more or less in isolation, for experience and delight. There are others whose poetry, though equally giving experience and delight, has a larger historical importance. Yeats was one of the latter: he was one of those few whose history is the history of their own time, who are part of the consciousness of an age which cannot be understood without them. This is a very high position to assign to him: but I believe that it is one which is secure.[2]

Over a decade later, Ezra Pound a friend of Yeats whose criticism of Yeats' poems c. 1908 had assisted the modernisation of the elder poet's style, was discussing poetry with a young admirer, Ronald Goodman.

> . . . Pound kept using the words 'major poet' in a way which seemed to exclude anyone who had not written an epic.
> 'But don't you think Yeats is a major poet?' [asked Goodman]
> Pound: 'Is he a Homer, is he a Dante?'
> Goodman: 'That's a mighty high standard.'
> Pound (laughing): 'I think Yeats is the greatest minor poet who ever lived!'.[3]

Part of the consciousness of the modern age? Greatest minor poet who ever lived? You will want to read all of Yeats' poetry before coming to a decision, but I hope this *Guide* has convinced you that his work is of a quality and scale to invite a debate at that level.

Notes

Chapter One

1 Letter of 14 March, 1888; in Wade, ed. *Letters*, p. 63.
2 J. M. Murry, 'Mr. Yeats's Swan Song' in *The Athenaeum*, 4 April, 1919; his review, together with many other reviews of Yeats's work between 1887 and 1939, is included in A. N. Jeffares, ed., *W. B. Yeats: The Critical Heritage* (1977), p. 218.
3 T. S. Eliot, 'A Foreign Mind' in *The Athenaeum*, 4 July, 1919; in *Critical Heritage*, p. 231.
4 J. G. Fletcher, review of *The Tower* in *The Criterion*, September 1928; in *Critical Heritage*, p. 287.
5 F. R. Leavis, *New Bearings in English Poetry* (1932; 1954), p. 46.
6 H. G. Porteus, review of *The Winding Stair* in *The Criterion*, January 1934; in *Critical Heritage*, p. 332.
7 T. S. Eliot, *After Strange Gods* (1934), p. 47; summarised in *Critical Heritage*, p. 231.
8 W. H. Auden, 'The Public *v.* the Late Mr. William Butler Yeats' in *Partisan Review* VI, 3 (Spring, 1939), pp. 46–51; included in the very useful anthology of criticism edited by Elizabeth Cullingford, *Yeats: Poems, 1919–1935*, which contains much other relevant criticism. (The quotation given is from the speech of the Counsel for the Defence, but it seems to carry authorial authority.)

Chapter Two

1 Yeats, *Essays and Introductions* (1961; 1974), p. 266.
2 Wade, ed., *Letters* (1954), p. 692.

Chapter Three

1 Details about publication can be found in Alan Wade's very useful *A Bibliography of the Writings of W. B. Yeats* (1951; revised 1958).
2 *A Vision* (1925; revised 1937; 1974), p. 279.
3 *Ibid.*, p. 280.
4 *Ibid.*, p. 68.
5 Ursula Bridge, ed., *W. B. Yeats and T. Sturge Moore: Their Correspondence 1901–1937* (New York, 1953), p. 162.

6   *Ibid.*

7   F. R. Leavis, in *Lectures in America* (1969), p. 67.

8   Frank Kermode, *Romantic Image* (1957), p. 85; in Cullingford, p. 219.

9   Y. Winters, *The Poetry of W. B. Yeats*, (Denver, Colorado, 1960), p. 14; in Cullingford, p. 129.

10. Leavis, *Lectures in America*, p. 78.

11   *Ibid.*, p. 79

12   Hugh Kenner, 'The Sacred Book of the Arts' in *Sewanee Review* LXIV, 4 (1956), reprinted in Kenner's *Gnomon* (New York, 1951; 1958), pp. 9–12; in Cullingford, p. 136.

13   *Ibid.*, in Cullingford, p. 138.

14   T. R. Henn, *The Lonely Tower* (1949; revised 1965), esp. Ch. 1. There is also a thorough study by the American scholar Donald Torchiana, *Yeats and Georgian Ireland* (Evanston, Illinois, 1966), though he lacks Henn's personal experience of the tradition.

15   Henn, *Lonely Tower*, p. 5; in Cullingford, p. 103.

16   *A Vision*, p. 52.

17   Donald Stauffer, 'The Reading of a Lyric' in *The Golden Nightingale* (New York, 1949); in Cullingford, p. 151.

18   G. Melchiori, *The Whole Mystery of Art* (1960), Ch. 3.

19   Yeats, *Variorum Poems*, p. 828.

20   See, for example, the stage directions to *At the Hawk's Well (1917)* in Yeats' *Collected Plays*, pp. 207, 218. It appears that in writing the poem Yeats created a composite image from paintings by Dulac and Cecil Salkeld; see Henn, *Lonely Tower*, p. 257.

21   In his Note to the 1921 volume *Michael Robartes and the Dancer* Yeats explained that he had written three earlier stories using the names Michael Robartes and Owen Aherne, and that he had decided to treat these as the names of friends to whom he would explain 'my philosophy of life and death' (p. 512). This he did in *A Vision*. In 'The Phases of the Moon' (pp. 183–8) the two figures discuss the vision the poet is developing in his lonely tower.

22   *A Vision*, p. 286.

23   D. Donoghue, *Yeats* (1971), p. 46.

24   *Ibid.*, p. 46.

25   *Ibid.*, p. 82.

26   *Ibid.*, p. 87.

Chapter Four

1   A. Wade, ed., *The Letters of W. B. Yeats* (1954); subsequently referred to as *Letters*. A more inclusive edition is currently in preparation; see John Kelly, ed., *The Collected Letters of W. B. Yeats*, Vol. I. 1865–1895 (Oxford, 1986)

2   *Letters*, p. 742; 25 April, 1928.

3   *Ibid.*, p. 740; 1 April, 1928.

4   *Ibid.*, p. 738; 23 February, 1928

5   *Ibid.*, p. 728; 2 October, 1927.

6   *Ibid.*, p. 760; 29 March, 1929.

7   *Ibid.*, p. 772; 16 December, 1929.

8 *Ibid.*, pp. 789–90; 3 January, 1932.

9 *Ibid.*, p. 814; 17 August, 1933.

10 *Ibid.*, p. 798; 30 June, 1932.

11 Thomas Parkinson has argued convincingly in *W. B. Yeats: The Later Poetry* (Berkeley, 1964), quoted in Cullingford, p. 135, that Yeats's use of formal stanzas – in this case not *ottava rima* but one derived from the seventeenth century poet Abraham Cowley used in Part II of 'The Tower' – was necessary 'chiefly ... as a discipline for the passionate syntax that he accepted as a norm'.

12 Harold Bloom, *Yeats* (London and New York, 1970), Ch. 20, quoted in Cullingford, p. 224.

13 *Ibid.*, p. 224.

14 *Ibid.*, p. 228.

15 See Donald Torchiana, *Yeats and Georgian Ireland* (Evanston, Illinois, 1966), esp. Chapters 4 to 8.

16 *Letters*, p. 810; 22 May, 25 May, 1933

17 According to Richard Ellmann, 'The Crazed Moon' was written as early as April 1923 (*The Identity of Yeats*, 1954; 1983, p. 291.) Its publication in 1933 suggests that Yeats felt it to be particularly relevant to current events.

18 See Daniel Harris, *Yeats, Coole Park and Ballylee* (Baltimore and London, 1974). Biographies of Lady Gregory include Elizabeth Coxhead, *Lady Gregory: a Literary Portrait* (1961) and M. L. Kohlfeldt, *Lady Gregory: The Woman Behind the Irish Renaissance* (1985). Lady Gregory herself published a small book entitled *Coole* in 1931.

19 See Donald Stauffer on Yeats's use of the swan image in *The Golden Nightingale* (New York, 1949), Ch. IV; in Cullingford, pp. 146–58.

20 The quotation is given in David Brewster, *Memoirs of the Life, Writings, and Discoveries of Sir Isaac Newton*, 2 vols. (Edinburgh, 1855), II, pp 407.

21 See p. 22 above.

22 *Ibid.*

23 G. S. Fraser, 'Yeats's "Byzantium"', *Critical Quarterly* II, p. 3 (1960), pp. 254–61; in Cullingford, pp. 207–17, esp. pp. 215–16.

24 Frank Kermode, *Romantic Image* (1957), p. 89; in Cullingford, p. 223.

25 F. A. C. Wilson, *Yeats and Tradition* (1958), p. 243.

26 Kenneth Burke, *A Rhetoric of Motives* (Berkeley, 1950; 1969), p. 317.

27 Finneran, *W. B. Yeats: The Poems* (1983), p. 659.

28 Wilson, *Yeats and Tradition*, p. 268.

29 Parkinson, *Yeats:The Later Poetry*, p. 57.

Chapter Five

1 Finneran's edition of the poems restores Yeats's order for *Last Poems*.

2 Frank Kermode, ed., *Selected Prose of T. S. Eliot* (London, 1975), p. 257.

3 Charles Norman, *Ezra Pound* (London, 1969), pp. 44–5.

Suggestions for Further Reading

There are many good books about Yeats. This list gives only a selection.

WORKS BY YEATS

This Guide is based on the Macmillan edition of *The Collected Poems of W. B. Yeats*, 2nd edition, 1950, and frequently reprinted.

R. J. Finnerman's *W. B. Yeats: The Poems — a New Edition* (Macmillan, 1983) includes a number of poems not in the earlier volume.

Autobiographies (Macmillan, 1955).

Collected Plays (Macmillan, 1953).

Essays and Introductions (Macmillan, 1961).

A Vision (Macmillan, 1925; revised 1937).

Collected Letters, ed., A. Wade (Macmillan, 1954).

Selected Plays, ed., A. N. Jeffares (Macmillan/Pan 1964, 1974). Paperback.

Selected Criticism and Prose, ed., A. N. Jeffares (Macmillan/Pan, 1980). Paperback.

WORKS ABOUT YEATS

Bibliography:

A Bibliography of the Writings of W. B. Yeats, ed. A. Wade, (Hart-Davis, 1951, 1958, 1968). A very useful tool.

Biography and Criticism:

Louis Macneice, *The Poetry of W. B. Yeats* (Oxford U.P., 1941). A Thirties view of the poetry.

Joseph Hone, *W. B. Yeats, 1865–1939* (Macmillan 1942; 1962). The standard life

T. R. Henn, *The Lonely Tower* (Methuen 1949; 1965). Particularly good on the Anglo-Irish element, and the visual arts, in Yeats.

A. N. Jeffares, *W. B. Yeats: Man and Poet* (Routledge 1949; 1962). Contains much material from Yeats's autobiographical papers.

R. Ellmann, *Yeats: The Man and the Masks* (Faber 1949, 1961). Biography with many critical insights.

R. Ellmann, *The Identity of Yeats* (Faber 1954; 1964). On Yeats's poetic development, with useful Appendix dating the poems.

Frank Kermode, *Romantic Image* (Routledge, 1957). Places Yeats in the Symbolist tradition.

F. A. C. Wilson, *Yeats and Tradition* (Gollancz, 1958). On Yeats's relationship to Neo-Platonism.

Georgio Melchiori, *The Whole Mystery of Art* (Routledge, 1960). Lively on Yeats's aesthetics.

A. G. Stock, *W. B. Yeats: His Poetry and Thought* (Cambridge U.P., 1961). Clear and level-headed.

C. K. Stead, *The New Poetic* (Hutchinson, 1964). Puts Yeats in his context.

Thomas Parkinson, *W. B. Yeats: The Later Poetry* (California U.P., 1964; 1972). Particularly interesting on Yeats's syntax.

A. N. Jeffares and K. G. W. Cross, eds., *In Excited Reverie* (Macmillan, 1965). A lively variety of essays published for the Centenary Year.

Donald Torchiana, *Yeats and Georgian Ireland* (Northwestern U.P., 1966). Thorough and informative.

Harold Bloom, *Yeats* (Oxford U.P., 1970). Powerful and eloquent.

Denis Donoghue, *Yeats* (Fontana, 1971). Brief but eminently perceptive.

A. N. Jeffares, ed., *W. B. Yeats: The Critical Heritage* (Routledge, 1977). Contains contemporary criticism of Yeats's works as published.

G. J. Watson, *Irish Identity and the Literary Revival* (Croom Helm, 1979). Excellent placing of Yeats with Synge, O'Casey and Joyce.

Elizabeth Cullingford, *Yeats, Ireland and Fascism* (Macmillan, 1981). An impressively temperate treatment of the controversial subject of Yeats's politics.

Gloria C. Kline, *The Last Courtly Lover* (U.M.I. Research Press, 1983). On Yeats's attitude to women.

Elizabeth Cullingford, ed., *Yeats: Poems 1919–35 (Macmillan, 1984)*. Contains extracts from the best criticism of Yeats's later work.

C. K. Stead, *Pound, Yeats, Eliot and the Modernist Movement* (Macmillan, 1986). A controversial, well-argued 'placing' of Yeats.

Index